Growing Pains

Growing Pains

Reflections on Life as a Teen

Glen Kuck

Publishing House
St. Louis

The Bible text in this publication is from the Good News Bible, the Bible in TODAY'S ENGLISH VERSION. Copyright © American Bible Society 1966, 1971, 1976. Used by permission.

Copyright © 1985 Concordia Publishing House
3558 S. Jefferson Avenue, St. Louis, MO 63118-3968
Manufactured in the United States of America

All rights reserved. No part of this publication may be reproduced, stored in a retrieval system, or transmitted, in any form or by any means, electronic, mechanical, photocopying, recording, or otherwise, without the prior written permission of Concordia Publishing House.

Library of Congress Cataloging in Publication Data

Kuck, Glen, 1950-
    Growing pains.

    Summary: Presents fifty readings reflecting the particular concerns of teenagers and discussing how the Gospel can form values, give guidance, and bestow self-esteem.
    1. Youth— Prayer-books and devotions — English. 2. Youth—Religious life. [1. Prayer books and devotions. 2. Youth—Religious life. 3. Christian life] I. Title.
BV4850.K83   1985   242'.63   85-7774
ISBN 0-570-03980-0

---

1 2 3 4 5 6 7 8 9 10 PP 94 93 92 91 90 89 88 87 86 85

To Cynde

Contents

Preface	11
Coping with Undeserved Love	13
Get Smart	15
One Life to Live	16
Gold Mines and Goal Minds	18
Beyond the Cosmos	19
Judgment Day for Ann	21
Living in the Twilight Zone	23
Mirror, Mirror on the Wall	25
The Case of the Enraged Teacher	27
Having Too Much to Do — and Loving It	28
Part-time Friends	29
The Making of an Ex-Christian	30
Being for Real	32
Does God Accept Credit?	34

The Art of Pessimism	36
That Old Gang of Mine	38
The Life and Times of an Unknown Man	40
A Tale of Two Sisters	42
People—the Real and the Phony	44
Prayer: How Do You Get It to Work?	45
Did Jesus Really Mean That?	47
Despair	48
Trying to Figure God Out	50
Acting Concerned vs. Concerned Action	52
Sitting Alone in the School Cafeteria	53
Life with Mother	55
Standing on the Shoulders of Giants	57
Are You Mr. Right?	58
Worship That's Worth It	60
The End?	61
Living in the Fast Lane	63
The Sadness of Beauty	64
Burying the Hatchet vs. Bearing the Hatchet	65

Another World	67
For Better or for Worse	68
Digging into the Past	70
Having Solitude as a Companion	72
A Case Study of Two Doctors	74
Getting Around the Law	75
From Here to Eternity	76
The Odd Couple	77
Mindless Guilt and Guiltless Minds	79
The Clockwork Universe	80
What Are Friends for, Anyway?	81
God's Eyes Never Blink	82
Easy Streets and Difficult Paths	84
Problems, Perplexities, and Parents	85
This Old House	86
The Road Not Taken	88
This Time Forever	89
In Closing	90

Preface

Samuel Butler once wrote, "Life is like playing a violin in public and learning the instrument as one goes on." He meant that people find themselves thrust into life and are told to live it. We have no chance to practice beforehand. Inevitably, mistakes are made. We get on-the-job training. We must learn as we go along.

Our predicament is complicated immensely because the circumstances around us keep changing. Just when we learn to cope with our present situation things change and new problems arise. The challenge before each of us is to prepare now for a future that will be far different from our present experiences.

The purpose of this book is not to provide concrete solutions to each of life's problems. Trying to do so would result in advice that is overgeneralized and simplistic. The problems of life are too complex to be solved with just a few bits of advice. This is especially true in a world that continues to change so rapidly. Solutions that seem to work one day may result in failure the next.

But as we begin to see that God, who cared enough to send His Son to die for us, longs to go through life with us, we begin to turn in the right direction. Because of Jesus' death and resurrection, paths that were previously closed to us are now open. The Gospel brings with it new and exciting possibilities. Our sins formerly put before us a road sign that said, "Do Not Enter." Christ's actions for us changed that sign to "Come On In." Opened to us now is a world filled with newness and excitement. It's a world of challenges — each of which can be approached with trust in the Lord.

If in the old and the new, the failures and the successes, the pains and the joys of each day we can cling by faith to this Good News, problems can become manageable. Life can become a meaningful venture. May this book help to strengthen your faith in Christ and the life-changing effect of His death and resurrection.

Coping with Undeserved Love

Happiness is the conviction that we are loved in spite of ourselves.
— *Victor Hugo*

It must have been stolen. Bill's three-day-old bicycle had been leaning up against the garage only an hour before. Now it was gone. Bill was more sad than angry. He'd have to do a lot more walking now. And he wouldn't have the 10-speed to show off anymore. But mostly Bill was sad because he remembered what his dad had said to him the day he got the bike. "Your mother and I spent a little more money on this than we had intended, but you're worth it. So be careful riding it, and take good care of it." Bill knew he had let his father down.

He decided to at least try to make up for it. He cleaned out the garage, took out the garbage, and did the dishes. When his dad got home that day, Bill told him what had happened. Dad was hardly amused, but he seemed to take it pretty well.

The day after the theft Bill noticed a new bike in the corner of the garage. Bill's brother, Andre, was having a birthday in a few days. Andre would like the new bike. It was a beauty.

Bill continued to do extra things for his parents like washing windows and cutting the grass. Each day he'd find some chores that Mom or Dad usually got stuck doing.

When Andre's birthday came, Bill was surprised that his parents had bought him a new video game cartridge. The new bike in the garage hadn't even been mentioned. Bill asked his dad about it. "Bill, that new bike's been in the garage for three days now," replied Dad. "Why haven't you been riding it? It's yours, you know."

Bill was stunned. Even though he had let his parents down by not caring for his bike, they bought him a new one. He could hardly believe it.

Then a new thought came to him. He had been doing extra work the past few days to make up for his mistake. The bike had been in the garage ever since the day after the theft. He wouldn't have had to do the work. He would have gotten the bike anyway.

But as he continued to ponder, Bill was glad he had worked extra hard. It had eased the work load for Mom and Dad. It was a good way of thanking them, even though he didn't know that's what he was doing at the time.

This story didn't happen just once. It's happened millions of times since history began. It happened long before bicycles were even invented. You see, this wasn't really a story about Bill, his parents, and two bikes. It was about people, God, and our abilities.

God gives each of us abilities. He asks us to use them responsibly. But we don't. We waste our gifts. We fall short of God's expectations for us. When we become aware of this, we may act like Bill. We may try to make up for our misdeeds by doing things to please God. But if we try to earn forgiveness through our actions, our attempts are futile. We can't put ourselves in a position of deserving forgiveness. Like Bill, we can only accept the free gift given us. In our case, this free gift is God's Son—sent to die for us. This gift is presented to us because of love, not because we deserve it.

It would have been understandable if Bill's father would have chosen not to replace his son's bike. Likewise, had God chosen not to send His Son, we would have no grounds on which to complain. The question then is this: Now that Christ took the punishment for our sins upon Himself, what are we to do with this undeserved gift?

In one of his letters to the people of Corinth, Paul talked about this. "He died for all, so that those who live should no longer live for themselves, but only for Him who died and was raised to life for their sake" (2 Corinthians 5:15).

Jesus' death for us means that we are now sinless in God's sight. Jesus suffered the punishment for us. We don't deserve such favorable treatment. Yet that's what we receive. Because of this, our lives are changed radically. We are now enabled to show people some of that love. We need no longer be trapped by the meaninglessness of attempts to serve only ourselves. We can now use our abilities to help those around us see Christ.

We can show love to others because of the love He first showed us. Doing so is a meaningful way of thanking God for the free gift of Christ.

Get Smart

The less you know, the more you think you know. The more you know, the less you think you know.
— Frank Hughes

Once upon a time a boy sat at his desk in the third row of the classroom. "Is a noun a word that shows action, or is it a verb that does that?" he asked himself. He stared at the English test in front of him, wishing he could remember. "Will I ever be smart enough to know the parts of speech?" he wondered.

A few years later he sat at home, pondering a quadratic equation. He had listened carefully to the teacher's explanation in class that day, but he was still having trouble. "I wish I understood this stuff better. Will I ever be smart enough?" he asked himself. He whispered a prayer, asking God for understanding.

Years passed. The table in front of him was cluttered with forms, receipts, statements of income, and tax schedules. The deadline for filing his income tax was fast approaching. But there was much that confused him. His wife didn't seem able to help much. "Will I ever be able to do this right?" he mumbled.

The years rolled on. He sat in his office at work. His employees had gone home for the day. It was late, but the payroll checks still had to be made out and signed by him. And there were decisions to be made about some future shipments. "Will I ever be intelligent enough?" he asked, as he stared at the picture on his desk. It was a picture of his two sons, dressed in their Little League uniforms. He then continued his work, praying that his decisions would be the right ones.

Years later he lay in a hospital bed. He had been there for a week. In his mind he tried to calculate the cost incurred by his hospital stay. He wanted to determine how much of it was covered by his insurance. But he had more questions about it than answers. "Will I ever know enough?" he mused.

Two days later he was dead. His wife, two sons, their wives, and their children mourned his death. They all loved him. He was a good man. He provided well for them and taught them much by his example and life of trust in the Lord. He had lived a long and productive life. The little boy who had trouble with nouns and verbs 50 years before had grown up to be a man. At each stage of his life he had encountered new problems. But he was always enabled to keep going.

He had been smart enough. God made sure of that.

One Life To Live

Too many people itch for what they want but they don't want to scratch for it.
— Will Rogers

Two boys walked to a neighborhood public swimming pool. The older boy climbed the ladder to the diving board, walked to the end of it, bounced up and down a few times, and dove in head first. A minute later he climbed out of the pool with a grimace, as if he were in pain. "I can't wait until Friday," he said.

The younger boy said nothing. He stood on the side of the pool and watched his friend ascend the ladder a second time. Again he dove into the pool. As he struggled out, he appeared to be shaken up a little. He repeated, "I can't wait until Friday."

"Why?" asked the younger boy. "What's so special about Friday?"

"That's the day they put water into the pool" was the reply.

Some people can't seem to wait to enjoy things. They don't want to put off pleasure, even for a few days. They need immediate gratification. Others seem better able to delay the experiencing of enjoyment, knowing that waiting will bring a more worthwhile result.

One boy may spend all of his weekly allowance at the video arcade while another saves his in order to some day buy the catcher's mitt he wants. Or one girl may fulfill her need for immediate pleasure by watching television all evening. Another girl puts off the enjoyment she could get from watching television in order to study for a test coming up in a few days. To her the rewards of a good test grade are greater than the temporary pleasure of a few television programs.

It's often necessary to do without short-lived enjoyment so that something more worthwhile can be achieved. The problem with momentary pleasure is that it comes, gives some enjoyment, then goes again. That's all there is to it—a fleeting moment of cheer. On the other hand, to attain something worthwhile may take some sacrificing, but the results are both longer lasting and more meaningful.

It's easy to agree that a person needs to delay immediate gratification in order to achieve certain goals. But it's often difficult to actually deny oneself. For example, pretend that a young man named Larry decided a few years ago to get a college degree. He knew it would take four years of hard work, but it's what he felt would be best for him. He was aware that whatever money he earned during those four years would have to be used to pay for his education. He accepted the challenge and went away to college.

Things were fine for a while. He liked his classes and he did fairly well. But when he returned home for the summer after his freshman year, he saw some of his old high school buddies. Ron worked at a gas station and Fred in a grocery store. Both of them had a lot more money in the bank than Larry. Both of them owned a car. All Larry had was the bills he owed for the next semester.

He returned to college the following fall. The classes seemed tougher. The costs increased. He wasn't able to work as much after his classes. He worried about passing his courses and having enough money to pay for them. He thought about his friends back home. They may not have been getting a college education, but they appeared to be far better off than he.

Now he wonders if a degree is really all that important. He could quit school, go home, probably find a job, pay his bills, and save up some money. What should he do? A college degree meant a lot to him at one time, but is it still worth the sacrifice?

The goals in life that are important enough to set are important enough to make sacrifices to attain. We need to trust that God is helping us to make intelligent decisions. We also need to feel that the goals we set for ourselves are worth the problems that they will bring. God gives us the ability to resist the need for immediate gratification that may block us from reaching long-range goals. We are thus able to impose upon ourselves the discipline to stave off the temptations that may get in our way. We know that the Lord will give us the strength to keep going. We trust that the rewards will be worth the sacrifice.

Gold Mines and Goal Minds

To travel hopefully is a better thing than to arrive.
— Robert Louis Stevenson

What happens when we set a goal, work hard to achieve it, make the necessary sacrifices, rely on God to help us, and then don't reach the goal after all? Have we failed? Has God failed?

Perhaps the use of an analogy is helpful. A runner is told that he will be in a race. He isn't told the length of the race, the course to be run, or the competition. In view of this, he can't very well set specific goals. He can't set a goal of finishing the course in, say, two minutes, because he has no idea of its length. He can't realistically expect to finish first if he has no idea of the competition. All he can do is train his body to run as efficiently as possible.

Life for us is similar to the plight of the runner. We don't know what to expect. Where life will lead, for how long it will last, and who will be encountered along the way are all unknowns. Therefore our goals can't always be very specific. We simply don't know what our circumstances will be in future years. About the only thing predictable about life is that it will bring the unexpected. To prepare well for such a vague future means to train oneself to live as meaningfully as possible.

It's tempting to wish that life could be more predictable. It would be nice to know that if we worked hard to reach a goal, that goal would always be reached. But life isn't like that, and maybe it's best that way. Perhaps such a predictable pattern of work, work, achieve ... work, work, achieve would get monotonous before long.

Often we find that once a goal is achieved it isn't quite as enjoyable as we had expected. Achieving one goal may only lead us on a quest to achieve another, hoping that the new goal will be more fulfilling.

There's an old saying that the rainbow is more beautiful than the pot at the end of it. It may be that the goal itself isn't as rewarding as the effort to achieve it. The end result isn't as enjoyable as the time spent in getting there. The experience of the rainbow is what is beautiful, not the pot itself.

It is in striving toward a goal that much is experienced. Mistakes are made and corrected, tears are shed and dried, and dreams are made, shattered, and made again. On the way to a goal we learn about ourselves. We discover the feeling of fulfillment that hard work gives. We find that there's something very right about self-imposed work and the discipline it teaches.

Life should not be spent trying to find the perfect job or spouse or car. That can only lead to disappointment. Instead, life should be lived in the never-ending desire to grow, to learn, and to improve. Preparing for a life filled with the unexpected takes both flexibility and stability. We need to be flexible, able to adapt to the changes that will be encountered. Stability is needed to stay unmoved and unshaken in our trust that God will do what is best for us.

Behind all of life's encounters is a God who cares. He didn't send His Son to die for us as some experiment to satisfy His curiosity or to just see what would happen. Jesus' life on earth was undertaken because we needed Him. Without His life, death, and resurrection we had no future. God does indeed care.

Being a Christian in a world such as ours means that we rely on that saving act as the "bottom line." It means that whether things turn out as we want them to or not, we are now and always will be forgiven children of God. Armed with this assurance, we can meet each of life's challenges confidently.

Beyond the Cosmos

I do not know what I may appear to the world, but to myself I seem to have been only like a boy playing on the seashore, and diverting myself in now and then finding a smoother pebble or a prettier shell than ordinary, while the great ocean of truth lay all undiscovered before me.

— Isaac Newton

Pretend that you are boarding a spaceship that will take you to the outer reaches of the known universe. Such a trip is, of course, impossible. But let's suppose it is feasible. Let's also suppose that you are able to stay alive long enough to finish the mission and can take along all the supplies you will need. Your spaceship is so fast that it can travel at the speed of light, about 186,000 miles per second. That's fast enough to go around the world seven times in just one second!

You begin your sight-seeing tour by flying toward the sun. Even though your spaceship is very, very fast, it still takes a full eight minutes to get there. As you approach the sun, you veer off and direct yourself toward the planet Pluto. Five hours later you whiz past this planet. You are now out of our solar system.

Your journey then takes you toward the nearest star other than the sun. It's called Alpha Centauri. After more than four years, still traveling at the speed of light, you finally near it. You are fascinated to see that Alpha Centauri is really three stars in orbit around each other. By now you have traveled a total of 25 trillion miles.

But your trip has hardly begun. Remember, you want to explore the outer reaches of the known universe. So you sit back and chart a course that will take you through the middle and out the other side of our galaxy.

As you approach the center, a reddish glow is given off by millions of older stars grouped together. You pass through that and steer toward the outer boundary of our galaxy. You'll have to be patient, though, since it will take your spaceship 80,000 years to get there.

By now you're totally overcome by the unspeakable immensity of God's creation. You ask how a God capable of creating the enormities of space can also create the details of a human being such as yourself. Your mind boggles as you look at a map that shows that your travels thus far are only a small fraction of the total trip you had envisioned. Beyond the Milky Way are clusters of galaxies. These, in turn, group together into superclusters. And, as enormous as these superclusters are, they are tiny compared to the total area of space. A trip to the ends of the universe as it is now known, you see, would take at least 20 billion years. You decide to turn back.

You're disappointed that you failed to accomplish your goal. The journey has made you more intensely aware of your human frailties and limitations. It is hard for you to deal with the thought that a God of such inestimable power could care so much for little, insignificant you. Why would Jesus ever want to become a member of humanity when He didn't have to, you ask. Why would He associate with inept, sinful people like me? Why would He ever be willing to die for me? You don't know. You can't understand, but you thank God that that's the way it is.

Judgment Day for Ann

Christ was without sin, but for our sake God made Him share our sin in order that in union with Him we might share the righteousness of God.

— 2 Corinthians 5:21

A One-Act Play

The scene is a huge, high-ceilinged, well-lit courtroom. The only furniture is the judge's bench. It is on a platform near the back wall. Behind it sits an imposing figure—an actor playing the part of God.

As the curtain is raised, an actress playing the part of Ann Smith is lead in by the bailiff. She enters hesitantly, obviously intimidated by the surroundings. Ann was a high school junior at the time of her death.

Bailiff: The judgment of Ann Smith will now begin.

God: Young lady, you are accused of disobedience of the Law. The Law can be summed up as follows: You shall love the Lord your God with all your heart, soul, and mind. And you shall love your neighbor as yourself.

I don't take any pleasure in telling you this, Ann, but you've failed miserably on both counts. The Law demands total commitment to Me, from which flows a concern for other people. But your attitude and actions on earth indicated that you were almost solely committed to yourself instead. You were concerned with yourself rather than with those around you who needed you. You were self-centered and tried to ignore those things that threatened to get in the way of your own interests. You made a god of yourself. Your attitude robbed not only me but the people with whom you lived as well. You hurt and scorned your friends. Your pride and superficial acts of goodness made you a hypocrite.

I trust, Ann, that you are aware of how very far you were from keeping the Law.

Ann: [After a long pause] Yes, Sir.

God: You took the gifts I gave you and treated them as if you deserved them. Not only were you ungrateful for all your blessings, you failed to share them with your neighbors. You therefore showed contempt for both Me and your fellow human beings. Once in a while you did some things to help those around you, but far more often you didn't.

Do you wish to refute what I have said, Ann?

Ann: No, Your honor.

God: In view of your disobedience of the Law I have no choice but to condemn you. The Law, your accuser, is very specific. It demands death—eternal damnation. It must be satisfied.

Ann: [Begins to speak but can think of nothing that will help her cause. She stands visibly shaken, her head down.]

God: Ann, I'm interested in why you chose to continually disobey the Law. You knew better, didn't you?

Ann: Yes Sir, Sir. Well ... I ... when I was on earth I knew I was a sinner. I knew I was disobeying the Law. I tried to do what was right. Honest, I tried. But I guess You were right in what You said about me letting my self-interests get in the way of what You had planned for me. I'm sorry ... but I guess it's too late for that.

God: Can you offer anything in your defense, Ann?

Ann: [After a heart-wrenching groan] No, Sir.

God: You know, Ann, I'm aware that while you were on earth you had faith in Christ's suffering, death, and resurrection. You trusted in His power over sin and its punishment, didn't you?

Ann: Yes, Your honor.

God: Why didn't you mention that when I asked if you had anything to offer in your defense?

Ann: I believed that Christ died for my sins. It's just that when I heard you read the Law's accusations it sounded so overwhelming.

God: You needn't sell Christ's work and your faith in that work so short. The Law's demands are great, but even greater is the love of Christ.

Ann: [Beginning to sound a bit hopeful] I did put my trust in Him, Sir. I really did.

God: [Smiling] I know you did, Ann. I told you before that the Law must me satisfied. It demands death for the criminal. I can't simply erase your name from my ledger of sins. I can't just overlook your sinfulness. But as you know, Jesus Christ came to earth to be sin for you. He took upon Himself the sentence for your sins. He lived a perfect life of obedience on earth. Yet He had to suffer all the torments of death. You know that wasn't easy for him, don't you?

Ann: Yes, Sir.

God: Because of His death, the demands of the Law have been satisfied.

Ann: [*Far more brightly*] Does that mean I'm innocent?

God: The Law's demands have been satisfied for you. You're free from the punishment you deserve because Christ took upon Himself the punishment of your sins for you. Your sins were put on the back of Jesus Christ. And while He took your sins upon Himself, He put His obedience on you. Now I consider you innocent.

Through faith, Ann, Christ's death became your death. The price has been paid. You and I are now in complete fellowship with each other, even though your sins separated us. We're once again in perfect harmony, just like I was with Adam and Eve before they sinned.

Bailiff, please escort this young lady into heaven, where she can be in unity with me and all the other believers forever.

I'm very happy for you, Ann.

As the curtain is lowered, Ann is making earnest attempts to thank God. But she is too shaken to even speak.

Living in the Twilight Zone

One death is a tragedy. A million deaths is a statistic.
— *Joseph Stalin*

There are two childhood diseases brought about by an acute lack of food. One is the result of not getting enough protein. It gives children bloated bellies and arms like matchsticks. The other is the result of an insufficient amount of calories. It makes babies look like wrinkled old people. Millions of children die each year from these diseases. Those who survive are often brain damaged or crippled.

Almost half a billion people in the world are at this moment either starving or undernourished. Twenty-seven thousand people will die today from starvation. Ten to twenty million die every year of disease due to malnutrition.

Statistics are safe. They are numbers on a page that can be conveniently shoved aside. But hunger isn't so easily put aside. It affects people who look and act and dream like us. It happens to real people, not numbers on a piece of paper.

It's almost useless to try to describe real hunger in words. Attempts become meaningless to those who have never experienced it. Hunger to a person who is starving is not at all like the desire for food that is commonly experienced by us. At first it is an all-pervading pain that gnaws at the entire being. The agony becomes inescapable. But later a numbness settles in on the body. A person seems to lose the ability to feel pain. One becomes hardly more than a lifeless form of flesh and bone.

Hunger is a tragedy. Somebody ought to do something about it, we say. And things have been done to alleviate world hunger. Organizations which render food aid around the world have been formed. The governments of wealthy countries have programs to dispense food, agricultural tools, and education. Experiments to grow more food are being conducted. But all of these efforts have been inadequate. The problem still persists.

We need to take matters into our own hands. But what can an individual do? Can one person really make a difference? The problem is not that an individual can't make a difference. It's that many of us are so involved in our own concerns that we fail to see the need. We aren't able to view things from a world perspective. We don't see the terrible imbalance between the haves and the have nots of this earth.

For example, while children in many parts of the world die from lack of protein, the average North American eats twice the recommended amount of protein he or she needs. People in North America use up 40 percent of this earth's disposable resources while they account for only 16 percent of the world's population. Obviously, then, one way to improve the imbalance is to better distribute the earth's wealth. But how can one person help to do this?

The problem of world hunger is so immense it may seem unalterable to the individual. But there are things that one human being can do that will help another human somewhere in the world.

Contributions can be made to world hunger organizations. A small amount of money goes a long way in feeding starving people.

Some individuals skip an occasional meal and then contribute the money that is saved by doing so. Such a plan helps the recipient of food but also helps the contributor to get a small, if only temporary, feeling for what it's like to be hungry.

New priorities can be established in the way we spend money. For instance, the money spent at a video arcade or for a new record album could instead be sent for the purchase of food.

Volunteer time can be given to either help begin or maintain a local food pantry. People donate food items and these foods are then distributed to those in need within the community. Hunger affects people in all corners of the world, including the corner at the end of the block.

The waste of food can be limited. It's been estimated that each year Americans waste about $5 billion worth of spoiled meat, fruit, and vegetables by simply buying too much at one time. Our society has built into itself an almost callous disregard for the scarcity of food in some parts of the world while we enjoy an overabundance. We often don't even give a second thought to food we throw away.

Solutions to the problems of world hunger begin with our attitude about human worth. We need to understand that the world was not put here for the personal satisfaction of us alone. Each of us is only one out of over four and a half billion people in the world. The material blessings we have are not only ours to use but ours to share. No one person can do everything to combat world hunger. But each of us can do things that will make a difference. Because of the feelings and actions of one, many lives can be enriched.

In a way our actions of helping those in need are somewhat like Christ's actions for us. And now, because we are related to Christ by faith, we find ourselves wanting to help those who are in need. Whatever we can give to someone else is a result of what Christ has given to us.

Mirror, Mirror on the Wall

The man who makes no mistakes does not usually make anything.
— Edward Phelps

A popular superstition is that one who breaks a mirror is in for seven years of bad luck. This belief dates back to a time long before glass mirrors existed. Early man, looking at himself in the calm waters of a pond, regarded his reflection as his other self. He believed that a disturbance occurring in the water would result in injury to this other self.

When polished metals and eventually glass began to be used for mirrors, this belief continued. If someone broke a mirror, it was assumed that bad luck would result. Later, the Romans decided that this bad luck would continue for seven years. The period of seven years was chosen because some medical theories at that time held that life renewed itself every seven years. Since a broken mirror resulted in injury to the other self, it was believed that recovery would take seven years.

Superstitions like this have no basis in fact. It is illogical to think that breaking a piece of glass could possibly result in the changing of one's future. But this superstition is an interesting one because of its origin. The theory of the existence of another self in addition to the real self deserves a further look.

It's natural for a person to view himself or herself as really two people. It's as if one of us is watching the other, quick to note how we're doing and especially what it is we're not doing well. This inner self knows us as no one else ever will. It knows all that we're doing and thinking. It gives us a continual evaluation.

For some people this other self may be a harsh, unforgiving critic. Our friends and acquaintances forgive and eventually forget our mistakes. But our inner self may not. It may continue to haunt us with memories of past wrongs.

Christians have learned that when the Lord forgives us, He forgives us completely. He wipes away all evidence of our sin. While it may do no harm to continue to express our sorrow for past misdeeds, we need to be convinced that we truly are forgiven. "I am telling you the truth: everyone who sins is a slave of sin," Jesus once said. "If the Son sets you free, then you will be really free" (John 8:34, 36). If, then, we are forgiven by God, we must then forgive ourselves.

Because we are sinful, we make mistakes, but we learn from them and go on with living. We go on with life, knowing that we'll continue to sin. We'll also continue to annoy our inner self. But we can feel assured that God's forgiveness is total forgiveness. Our sins, which once made us deserving of God's wrath, are now, because of Christ, erased. We are indeed free.

The Case of the Enraged Teacher

Swallow your pride occasionally. It's nonfattening.
— Frank Tyger

Here's the scene: It's a warm Thursday afternoon. The windows throughout the school are open. Your last class of the day has just ended. You are walking past Mr. Smith's classroom toward your locker. You notice that the wind is blowing some papers he had stacked on his desk onto the floor. No one else is in the room at the time, so you decide to do Mr. Smith a favor. You pick up the scattered history tests and put them back on the desk. Just as you finish stacking them, Mr. Smith enters.

"What are you doing with those tests?" he yells.

"I was just—the wind was blowing . . . ."

"No student is supposed to be in here now. How do I know you weren't changing your test answers or looking in my desk?"

"All I was doing was gathering up the tests that the wind was blowing onto . . ."

"I heard you say that before. Well, I won't report this even though I should. I had better not catch you in here alone again. Now get out of here."

You feel misunderstood, helpless, and angry. But what do you do? You have some options. You could stay there until Mr. Smith listens to you story. But he's certainly not in a listening mood right now.

You could walk out and say either to yourself or to him that you'll never try to help him again. This may not help matters, but at least it will make you feel a little better.

You could walk out and try to forget the incident. That won't be easy.

Or you could walk out without a word but arrange some way of getting even. If nothing else you could get some revenge by telling your friends what happened and how stupid Mr. Smith was for acting the way he did.

Again, what do you do? One's natural inclination is to get even in some way for the injustice. It would feel good to teach Mr. Smith a lesson. After all, you were just trying to help him out a little, and then he started yelling at you. But getting even would take some daring, since he's the teacher and can probably get you into a lot of trouble.

Perhaps, however, the action that takes the most courage is the one in which you do nothing. Taking an injustice without releasing a volley of vindictive words or actions of your own requires much inner strength. A great degree of maturity is needed to accept the mistake of Mr. Smith. A lot of foresight is required to see that any act of vengeance on your part would be counterproductive.

St. Augustine once said, "If you are suffering from a bad man's injustice, forgive him lest there be two bad men." Forgiving costs you nothing. It's often difficult, it's unconventional, but it's best.

Having to Much to Do— and Loving It

When people are serving, life is no longer meaningless.
— John Gardner

"I like the money coming in from my after-school job, but it really cuts into my study time. I've got two tests coming up on Friday, and I haven't even started to study for them yet. And I promised I'd help Angie with her term paper. It's due next week. Now Mom wants us to help clean up the house for Uncle Frank's visit tonight. I just wish there were more hours in a day."

Valerie listened as her sister, Kisha, continued to tell her how busy she was. Kisha took her schoolwork seriously, and she was worried now that she was falling behind. She wanted to stay up late and study after Uncle Frank left, but she knew she'd be too tired by then. She would love to take a few days off from her after-school job. She wished she didn't have so much to do and could just relax, watch TV, and do nothing for a few days. But these were just wishes, not reality.

That evening Kisha listened as her uncle told her family about how he had been spending his time lately. His employer had gone out of business. He had been looking for work, but few companies were interested in hiring him. "I'm not getting any younger, and employers are looking for younger men. I know I can do the work if they'd give me the chance, but I just can't get one.

"About the only thing I've been doing lately is filling out applications and then going home and watching TV. That gets boring before long. Sometimes I just wish each day was a few hours shorter. Time just drags on so slowly when there's nothing to do. It seems to take an eternity for night to come. But then when it's time to go to bed I can't sleep. After not doing anything all day, I'm just not sleepy. So I lie awake and worry. Just sitting around the house with nothing to do is tough. It's probably the hardest thing I've had to do in my life."

As she listened, Kisha thought about her job, her tests, and the term paper. Somehow she didn't feel so overwhelmed by them anymore. She began to realize how fortunate she was to be busy.

Part-time Friends

You can always tell a real friend: when you've made a fool of yourself he doesn't feel you've done a permanent job.
— Laurence J. Peter

Ralph was thinking about his best friend, Steve. They had known each other for about five years. No one was more concerned for Ralph's well-being than good old Steve. They had shared a lot of times together, both good and bad. They had hiked and fished and played ball with each other for years now.

There were times when Ralph wanted to let Steve know how much he appreciated having him as a friend. But he just couldn't find the words to express himself. So he said nothing.

But as much as Ralph appreciated Steve, there was one thing about him that really aggravated Ralph. Whenever a girl came by, Steve became a different person. He'd try to act clever and witty, hoping to impress the girl. He'd become so engrossed in his conversation with the girl that Ralph would feel as if he wasn't even there. Not once would Steve introduce Ralph to his female friends. And whenever Ralph would do something to be noticed, Steve would just ignore him. When girls were around, it was as if Ralph didn't exist.

Ralph could never understand how a normally concerned, caring person like Steve could become so rude. Couldn't Steve understand what he was doing? Didn't he see how he was hurting his friend?

The two walked side by side toward Steve's house. Nothing was being said. This would be a good chance for Ralph to bring up the subject. If only Steve was told, maybe the problem would end. Steve must learn that others have feelings too. Yet Ralph didn't say anything about it. He just couldn't tell Steve. He'd have to hope Steve would figure out for himself how destructive humans can be when they become self-centered. They hurt others. They fail to fulfill their responsibilities as inhabitants of God's earth.

The two arrived at the house. Steve went inside and Ralph walked into the backyard. He lapped at the water dish, barked at a neighborhood cat, and walked into his doghouse. He then took a nap.

The Making of an Ex-Christian

Christianity is a life much more than a religion.
— R. M. Moberly

A boy once decided to someday become a professional baseball player. He began by playing softball whenever possible with his friends in the neighborhood. He played on his grade school team. He loved the game. He could seemingly never get enough of it. When it would get too dark to play outside he would go to his room to watch a game on television. He kept statistics on the performance of his favorite team. He read the sports section of the newspaper each day to find out whatever he could about his heroes.

When he got to high school he played on the baseball team. He was not a regular in the lineup, but he still loved the game. By the time he was a junior his interest in playing the game had waned, but his interest in keeping statistics had grown. He became the team statistician. Armed with his trusty calculator, he would evaluate each player's performance in terms of batting average, runs batted in, runs scored, and stolen bases. He was good at what he did. Statistics became his passion.

The once-important goal of playing baseball professionally had drifted into the background. By the time he graduated, he seldom even picked up a bat anymore.

A boy grew up as a Christian. At a young age he was captivated by the stories of Biblical characters. He loved the Lord and the study of His Word. He could seemingly never hear enough of Him. When it wasn't time for Sunday school or church or devotions, he read whatever he could about God and His love for people. He devoted his life to being a Christian.

The boy went on to high school. His knowledge of the Bible continued to increase. He impressed many people with the facts he knew about the Bible and his ability to debate Biblical interpretations. Armed with this knowledge and his gift for speaking, he was quick to offer his evaluation of any sermon or theory about God.

In college, the study of philosophy became his passion. The once-important goal of living the life of a Christian faded into the background. He became progressively less concerned about his relationship to God. His only concern was the study of Christianity as a religious philosophy. By his senior year in college he seldom even said a prayer anymore.

The study of the Bible is essential. It is a never-ending source of wisdom and inspiration. But for some it has become little more than a source of quiz questions. It is something with which to impress people if enough knowledge about it is gathered. For some, knowledge about Bible history or the ability to speak profoundly about a Biblical topic has replaced growth in relation to God. Christ's work of redemption is all but forgotten.

Possessing a lot of Biblical knowledge no more makes a person a Christian than knowing a lot of baseball statistics makes a person a great baseball player. The continuing study of God's Word is vital to growth in faith. But it is not the end in itself. Too often God becomes the object of scholarly debate rather than the object of faith. To have faith in the Lord means to believe that He is in fact God and to stake one's life upon that claim. It is a trust that despite our failures and unworthiness, Christ's death in our place has set us right with God. From such belief, then, flow the thoughts, words, and actions that reflect this faith. We either acknowledge God as the essence of life itself or we reject Him. If we acknowledge Him, our lives can't help but be changed by this.

Christianity is not just a matter of the head, or even just a matter of confessing certain beliefs. It is a way of living. When Jesus lived on earth, His intention was not to begin a scholarly club whose goal was to establish a neatly organized system for categorizing religious teachings. Instead, Jesus began a movement—a new way of viewing life. He spoke about the kingdom of God as being governed by love. This love is first shown by God in Christ; then it is reflected in the kindness of humans toward each other as they live out their faith in Him. This movement sees the plight of people. It sees the suffering, the hunger, the loneliness, and the fears of fellow human beings. It sets out to do what is possible to end those things.

Faith is not knowledge only. Nor is it the mindless repetition of creeds and prayers. It is a total dependence on God and His mercy. As Christians we often have feelings of desperation, since we know that by ourselves we are helpless. But we also experience feelings of joy when we trust in Christ, in what He has done and continues to do for us. We move ahead in life as we live out our faith through greater closeness to Him and to His people.

Being for Real

We must have courage to bet on our ideas, to take the calculated risk, and to act. Everyday living requires courage if life is to be effective and bring happiness.

— Maxwell Maltz

One of Aesop's fables is about a tortoise that asked an eagle to teach him to fly. The eagle tried to talk him out of it, explaining that the tortoise lacked the physical requirements for flight. But the tortoise kept after him until he consented. Reluctantly, the eagle grabbed the tortoise with his talons and flew high into the sky. He then let go. Not being able to fly, the tortoise plummeted to earth. He crashed against some rocks and was dashed to pieces.

Aesop's fable was not written to expose the foolishness of tortoises. Its purpose was to show what can happen to humans who attempt to be something they are not. It illustrates the results of so-called bravery that is senseless.

Throughout history people have attempted many daring deeds, not because of the value in the acts themselves, but because of the apparent glory involved. It seems that competition for the attention and admiration of others has been, and still is, intense.

Perhaps it is helpful to consider what courage is and what it is not. Courage is not riding a bicycle in heavy traffic with no hands on the handlebars. Courage is not offering to fight someone over some meaningless matter of pride. Courage is not getting into drugs to conform to the expectations of others. Often an act that is labeled courageous is instead simply a chance taken to show how daring one can be. It is motivated by a desire for attention or prestige. It accomplishes little, if anything. It brings out the phoniness in a person.

Courage is defending someone when the "in" thing to do is to ridicule that person. Courage is speaking out against what is wrong. It involves a willingness to be detached from what everyone else is doing—if what everyone else is doing is inappropriate. Courage involves taking a risk in an effort to help improve the plight of someone else, or even oneself. It involves difficulty and maybe danger. It is done with faith in Christ, not always knowing exactly how things will turn out. Courage brings out the best in a person. At times courage means not doing what others are doing. At other times it means doing what others are not.

To be oneself, to be real, is essential. In a time when too many people both young and old simply go along with the wishes and traditions of the majority, being oneself is a challenge. Being committed takes courage. The call of Christ makes those who respond to it commit themselves totally. We either follow the call or we don't. There's no middle ground. To follow this calling demands a courage to go beyond the normal expectations of the crowd. It demands a commitment to do what we can to let others see in our lives the difference Christ's death has made for us. The world of the Lord Jesus is a world no longer governed by the powers and traditions of past injustices. It's a world of change and of courage.

Christians are brave people by virtue of the power given them through Christ. But they aren't brave so that they can receive the praise or acceptance of peers. They're brave because of the difference that Jesus' life, death, and resurrection has made.

Paul, a man with more than a normal amount of courage, gives evidence of this in Philippians 4:13. He says, "I have the strength to face all conditions by the power that Christ gives me." Armed with Christ, we too can be courageous. That's really the only kind of life worth living.

Does God Accept Credit?

Christ died for men precisely because men are not worth dying for; to make them worth it.

— C. S. Lewis

Mr. Bennett had been teaching high school composition classes for 35 years. He was strict and demanding. He expected nothing less than perfection from his students. Each week a composition was assigned, graded, and returned. Mr. Bennett was unrelenting in his grading. "The rules of grammar must be followed precisely," he was often heard saying. Unless the students' writing conformed to all the rules, little credit was given. Many students failed his course.

Jack was worried. Each week he dutifully turned in a composition and each time it came back cluttered with corrections and criticisms. His spelling was poor. His grammar was weak. His sentence structure left much to be desired. Try as he might to find some way for his writing to please the instructor, the results were always the same. Jack simply was not passing the course.

He needed to do something. He found out that Mr. Bennett's son had written a few books. Jack found a copy of one of them and read it. The next day Jack arranged to stroll through the hallway with Mr. Bennett after school. Jack mentioned the book and how much he had enjoyed reading it. He said he thought Mr. Bennett's son was an excellent writer. In the future, he said, he would try to emulate his son's style. Jack buttered up his teacher as much as possible without being too obvious.

Jack's hopes for Brownie points hinged on his ability to impress Mr. Bennett with his statements about his son. Jack was gambling that what he said he believed would sway his teacher's opinion about his course grade.

Could the strategy really work? Probably not. Jack's writing didn't follow the rules of good writing. He deserved poor grades. His plan to earn credit points with Mr. Bennett could hardly be expected to work. A real-life teacher wouldn't allow himself to disregard the rules of grammar simply because of what a student said he believed.

As implausible as the plan was, it was similar to some people's approach to earning God's favor. The approach is as follows: We know God's law condemns us. It is constantly pointing an accusing finger at us. Like Jack and the rules of grammar, we are told repeatedly of our failures. We have often heard that those who believe in what Jesus has done for them are forgiven. So we confess our belief in Jesus' saving action and feel that we are at peace with God. We feel that our belief has earned us our salvation. We have said to God essentially what Jack said to Mr. Bennett. We hope that God's opinion of us can be swayed.

The problem with that approach, though, is that it makes it seem as if belief is a way for us to earn God's favor. It makes people appear able to save themselves. This approach pictures God looking down from above at people, searching for a sufficient degree of belief. If He finds it, He is satisfied and the entrance requirements to heaven have been met. We have, in effect, saved ourselves. But God hardly views things in this manner.

The good news of Jesus' death and resurrection, the Gospel, is not just something that makes up for people's inability to obey God's law. Believing that Jesus died and rose does not earn credit points with God. Our salvation cannot come as a result of gathering enough Brownie points through our actions or our beliefs. The Law is too overwhelming for that. Its demands can never be met by us.

Instead, the Gospel puts an end to the power of the Law's accusations. The Law's voice has been silenced because the Law's demands have been met. Jesus came to earth, lived under the Law, and fulfilled it for us. Jesus' life and death have made a new beginning for us. This new start enables us to carry on with our lives in the freedom He intended for us. The Law's stranglehold on us has been broken.

All of this has been accomplished for us by Jesus. We cling to it by faith. We live a life of trust in what has been done for us. We do nothing, however, to earn it for ourselves. God creates this faith in us. It is God's gift, given out of love for us.

We continue to sin. The Law keeps accusing us and showing us that we've failed miserably. But each day the Gospel comes to our rescue. God forgives our deficiencies and puts us at peace with Himself once more.

The Art of Pessimism

*'Twixt optimist and pessimist The difference is droll;
The optimist sees the doughnut,The pessimist, the hole.*
— McLandburgh Wilson

The salesman drove along the two-lane road, thinking about how badly his day had been going. He had spent two hours on the road and another three hours talking to purchasing agents. But he had made no sales. No one wanted to sell his product in their store. Now he was on his way to another town to try again. Things probably won't go any better there either, he thought.

It was mid-afternoon as the salesman spotted a weatherbeaten sign by the side of he road. It read simply "Pessimismville." As he slowed his car he couldn't help but notice the boarded up windows on many of the houses. He was hungry and had plenty of time before his appointment in Greentown, a little farther down the road. He saw a cafe and decided to stop. He entered the dimly lit room and sat at the counter. A sad-eyed waitress walked over to him. She stood silently.

"I'd like to order a hamburger."

"You might like to order one, but I doubt if you'll like to eat it," she mumbled. The salesman chuckled politely.

After she relayed the order to the cook, she returned to the counter. She didn't appear to be very busy, so he decided to strike up a conversation.

"It sure is a beautiful day outside."

"It'll probably rain."

The man turned to look out the window, "But there's not a cloud in the sky!"

"Believe me, mister, sooner or later it'll rain."

The salesman was relieved when she walked back into the kitchen. Soon another customer came in and sat down at the counter.

"Say, how long will it take me to drive to Greentown from here?" The salesman knew it was about 10 miles, but he thought that the question would be a way to break the silence.

The man lit his pipe and drawled, "Oh, probably about three or four hours."

"Three or four hours? I thought Greentown was only about 10 miles from here."

"It is, but the towing service here is awfully slow."

The salesman was quick to reply, "Why would I need a tow? My car runs fine."

"If you say so, stranger. But you never can tell."

The salesman fidgeted with the silverware. The waitress soon returned with the hamburger. "Do you want something to drink?"

"Yes, coffee."

"Want cream and sugar with it?" she asked.

"Yes, please."

"Good decision," chimed in the other customer, "that'll help to kill the taste of the coffee."

After a few minutes of silence the salesman decided to try again with the customer. "How come so many windows are boarded up around here?"

"I guess people just got tired of looking out."

"But why? The farmland is so beautiful in this area. It seems to me people would want to look out at the lovely scenery."

The customer relit his pipe. "Sure, it's nice now. But wait until the drought comes and the farmers' crops shrivel up."

The salesman couldn't believe his ears. "But the waitress just told me it rains a lot around here."

"It does, but only on people, not on the crops."

By now the salesman had had enough of his hamburger and his conversation. After paying his bill he started for the door. The waitress called out, "Come back again sometime. But I don't suppose you'll want to."

No, I don't suppose I'll want to, thought the salesman.

As he walked toward his car, he noticed a boy crying. The boy looked as though he was on his way home from school. The salesman walked up to him. "What's the matter, son?"

"I'm gonna get all Fs on my report card next month."

"How do you know? Did you teacher tell you that?"

Fighting back the tease, the boy responded, "No, she told me I was doing real good in school."

The salesman was stumped. "Then why do you think you'll get such a bad report card?"

"Because things are bound to get worse." The boy turned and walked away.

As the salesman drove away, he thought about the town and people of Pessimismville. Why was everyone so cheerless? It seemed as though no one had any hope. All they could do was to look on the negative side of life. It was almost as if they got pleasure from that. The man couldn't get those people out of his mind. There was something haunting about them. It was as if he had experienced them somewhere before. He knew he had never been to Pessimismville before. Yet he felt like he had just seen a rerun. Who had he known that overlooked the blessings only to view the negatives like those people did?

A few miles farther down the road it came to him. He realized why the words of those people sounded so familiar. He remembered who it was that so often spoke and acted as if there was no hope. It was he himself.

That Old Gang of Mine

Each time a man stands up for an ideal, or acts to improve the lot of others, or strikes out against injustice, he sends forth a tiny ripple of hope ... and crossing each other from a million different centers of energy and daring those ripples build a current that can sweep down the mightiest walls of oppression and resistance.

— Robert F. Kennedy

One of the great world leaders of the first half of our century was Mahatma Gandhi. While he labored mainly to free India from British rule and to correct injustices in India, his message spoke to an entire world.

There were four major castes, or social classes, in India's Hindu society. The *Brahmans* were the highest class. These were the priests and religious leaders. Next were the *Kshatriyas*, the warriors and princes. Third were the *Vaisyas*, who were the merchants and businessmen. The lowest caste was made up of *Sudras*, who were craftsmen and artisans. Members of one class could not move up into another class. Generation after generation lived within the same class.

The people who didn't belong to any of these four groups were called untouchables. They were given the dirty jobs such as sanitation and scavenging chores. These untouchables were not part of the caste system. They were below it. They were the outcasts.

In 1955, seven years after Gandhi's death, laws were finally passed which made discrimination against the untouchables illegal. Slowly, their plight began to improve. But while the historic injustices to this class continue to disappear today, the system of separating people by caste is still practiced. People still marry almost solely within their class. Children are unable to move up the social ladder. A child inherits the vocation and social position of his or her parents, just as the parents did from their parents.

It's unfortunate that such a system continues in India. It breeds feelings of resentment and superiority which shouldn't exist. But India isn't the only place where such attitudes can be found. They occur in our society as well.

For example, Ron hoped to be a part of the group of friends that included Mark and Joe. He really didn't want to go out for the football team like they did, but at least that way he had a better chance of being one of the guys. Ann spent long hours studying for each quiz and test. She wanted to make the Honor Society. By doing so she might be accepted by some of the members already in that group. Dan would have liked to be a good friend of Jeff. But Jeff didn't want to be seen with Dan, since he was a junior and Dan was only a freshman.

While our society talks about the individual's freedom to advance, it still builds barriers to restrict such movement. Societies have been guilty of such discrimination through the ages. If, through heredity or achievement, people attain a certain high level, they are often reluctant to let many others share that position. They feel a policy of exclusion will help to make others think more highly of them.

But such an approach hurts people. It builds unnatural barriers. It keeps us from being the homogeneous group God created us to be. Jesus spent much of His time on earth trying to get people to understand that. He lived and worked among the less fortunate, the social outcasts. While the sinful world is a world of classes and discrimination, Jesus' world is one of unity of purpose and spirit.

St. Paul wrote about the oneness of Christians in Galatians 3:28. When applied to our situation today, it might read as follows: There is no difference between Jews and Gentiles, between men and women, between athletes and nonathletes, between good students and poor, between freshmen and juniors; you are all one in union with Christ Jesus.

The Life and Times of an Unknown Man

*Because I could not stop for Death,
He kindly stopped for me;
The carriage held but just ourselves
And immortality.*

— Emily Dickinson

His name was John. He grew up working on his parents' farm. There wasn't much money to be made on the farm, and the hours were long. But at least the family had enough to eat. John learned a lot about life and about himself during the long hours alone in the fields.

By his mid-teens, John was doing the work of a man. His daily work would begin and end with the rising and setting of the sun. The farm was small, but there was always work to be done. The livestock needed to be cared for, and crops had to be planted, cultivated, and harvested. John didn't have much chance to attend school. Back then a formal education wasn't considered essential.

When he was 17, his mother died. She was only 39. Two years later, his father passed away. John was on his own, left with the farm and its mortgage payments due each month.

For the first few years the wheat and corn harvest was good. There was plenty of winter work for him in town as a bricklayer. He was able to meet his mortgage payments. And he even met a girl. The two of them were married when he was 22. His wife kept the garden and sold some produce in town. The extra money helped, because farm prices were low. Not many folks were building houses, so there wasn't much bricklaying work to be done either.

The Depression had come. Things didn't cost much to buy, but it hardly mattered to John, since he didn't have enough money anyway. Rain was scarce in 1933. The money he got for selling his crops amounted to almost nothing. It was tough trying to keep his family from hunger. There were now three daughters. John knew it wasn't his fault that the kids didn't have much to eat, but he couldn't help but feel guilty. He kept thinking he should be a better provider.

Selling the farm became imperative. He didn't get much money for it, since few others had much money to spend either. But at least now there was a little money and an end to the mortgage payments. The five of them had a house, a garden, their health, and their trust in the Lord. John and his wife never forgot to show their kids how much the Lord meant to them.

Jobs were hard to find, and like many others, John was without work for some time. But eventually an opening came up in town for a bricklayer. Old Tom Lindsay had died and Mr. Jenkins needed a bricklayer to take his place. John was given the job with only the promise that the hours would be long and the pay would be low. But John was happy. Many of his friends had no job at all.

When the war broke out, the economy began to improve. Factories needed to be built and good bricklayers were in short supply. John was working almost as much as when he was on the farm. He worked six days a week all year around. A vacation would have been nice after a while, but it couldn't be afforded.

His daughters were growing fast. Emily was 14 now. Watching her and her two smaller sisters was worth the long hours of labor for John. He wanted the best for them. They were an important part of his life.

He worked for 18 more years as a common laborer for Mr. Jenkins. John was now in his mid-fifties and wasn't as strong as he had once been. He was thankful when old Mr. Jenkins made him a foreman. But John wasn't very good at giving orders. He usually did the work himself instead of assigning it to others. His last few years on the job weren't so happy. He was looking forward to retirement. He never made it. He died at the age of 59.

Who was this guy named John? It's not important. He never became famous. He's not written about in any history book. Few people other than his relatives even remember him now.

Was John's life even worth living? Of course it was. As a result of his work, buildings were constructed and people were fed. Children learned from his example. His daughters were able to get the good education John had worked so hard to insure. John's small corner of the world was made better because of hard work and faith in the Lord.

Much of what we in the 1980s have is due to the labors of our predecessors. Our institutions, factories, government, food, and chance for leisure are here because of the work of common people. Most of them are forgotten now. That's unfortunate, because so many of the blessings we enjoy today are given us because of the anonymous contributions of people like John. They have done the work of the Lord, never gaining fame, or even wanting it. The good things a civilization enjoys aren't so much the product of famous leaders. Rather, they are the result of dedicated, common men and women whose efforts reflect their faith in Christ.

To the degree they were able, they have succeeded in accomplishing what God expects of each of us. "God has made each of us what we are," Paul writes, "and in our union with Christ Jesus He has created us for a life of good deeds, which He has already prepared for us to do" (Ephesians 2:10).

The price that had to be paid for us to be forgiven was extraordinarily high. It cost Jesus His life. As we trust in Jesus as our Savior, we are reminded of this cost. We cannot simply accept His saving act and not be changed by it. To do so would be not to accept His love at all. With faith comes a commitment on our part. We have a responsibility as forgiven people of God to make our world a better place in which to live. We do so by giving tirelessly of our time and talents.

Like John, a Christian's concern is not only for himself or herself but also for those who need his or her help. Fame and fortune are not the goals a Christian strives for but—if God grants them—instruments to be used in serving God and our fellow human beings.

A Tale of Two Sisters

Love looks through a telescope; envy through a microscope.
— Josh Billings

A wise man told this story to a group of people seated around him:

Once upon a time there were 16-year-old twins named Stephanie and Lisa. Besides their looks, they shared the same interests, friends, likes, and dislikes. Both got good grades and planned to go on to college.

As their junior year in high school began, a new girl named Pam entered the picture. She lived next to one of Stephanie and Lisa's mutual friends. So she began to be included in their circle of friends. Pam became popular almost overnight. Her pleasing personality made her easy to get to know and like. Everything seemed so effortless for her.

Stephanie learned to like Pam and was glad to see how quickly she had adjusted to a new school. She was especially impressed by how smart Pam was in class.

On the other hand, Lisa was less than pleased. She was put off by Pam's good looks and good grades. She resented seeing some of the boys she admired become attracted to Pam. "Who does this newcomer think she is? First she tries to be friendly with me; then she steals my friends," Lisa thought to herself. Lisa had to admit that Pam had done nothing to directly hurt her. She just felt that Pam's rising popularity would hurt hers.

Pam's increasing popularity soon became a major issue in Lisa's life. She found herself trying to put Pam down in every conversation with others. She could think of little else. Before this year, life at school had been enjoyable. Now it was anything but enjoyable. That was all Pam's fault too, according to Lisa.

When the twins talked together at home, the discussion soon centered on Pam. Lisa couldn't understand how Stephanie could just go on with her own life and continue to be herself. How could she like Pam? Stephanie, on the other hand, couldn't understand how one new girl could upset Lisa so.

The wise man stopped for a moment. Finally he asked, "Which of these girls, then, do you judge to be truly happy?"

The group agreed that Stephanie's ability to be content and to be happy for someone else's good fortune had led to happiness for her. They realized that Lisa had destroyed herself through jealousy.

"Wait a minute, old man," came a voice from the back of the crowd. "You asked which girl was truly happy. I don't know about the rest of you, but I wouldn't want to be Stephanie or Lisa. I'd rather be Pam. Instead of just being content with the situation like Stephanie, I'd rather have Pam's looks and personality. She's the one that was truly happy."

The wise man smiled and said softly, "I'll go on with my story." He then told the group that life wasn't so great for Pam after all. Sure, she was popular with the friends of Lisa and Stephanie. But she wasn't content with that. She wanted to be a part of another group. That's where the really popular kids were, Pam thought. It became a consuming passion, trying to impress girls like Karen and Ann and the guys they knew. It was a never-ending feeling of discontent for Pam, not pleased with what she had and not able to obtain more.

The wise man's story was ended. The voice in the back of the crowd was silent. The listeners walked away.

People—the Real and the Phony

It is only by forgetting yourself that you draw near to God.
— *Henry David Thoreau*

A well-dressed man rang the doorbell of a minister's home and asked to see the pastor's wife. She was known for her efforts to assist needy people financially.

Trying to hold back his tears, the man blurted out the story of a poor family he knew. The father had left, the mother was sick, and the six children had very little food to eat. The family would soon have to be turned out into the cold of winter unless someone could pay their $150 monthly rent bill for them.

The lady put her hand to her mouth. "Oh, how awful. May I ask who you are?"

Holding his handkerchief close to his eyes, he sobbed, "I'm their landlord."

Shaking his head in disgust, the campaign manager gave the congressman his analysis. "The survey shows you're not very popular in the inner city. The people there don't think you care about them. You're going to have to make some speeches in that area. Tell them what they want to hear. It's the only way you can win reelection."

A few days later the congressman stood at the podium. He was ending his speech. ". . . I stand here this fine day, among the people I love and care about. I ask you to help me work toward those goals I established in my first term of office. I have worked to make this area of our great city among the finest anywhere. You people are my number one priority. I vow to continue my ceaseless efforts to help you in every way possible. Vote for someone who cares about you. Vote for someone who will work day and night for you."

He stepped down from the stage. The thought of all those extra votes brought a smile to his face. He left that area of town, not to return until the next election.

"Hi, Mrs. Anderson. Here are some cookies I baked for you and your kids," Tracy said as she stepped into the house.

"Well, that's very considerate of you. You've certainly been good to us. It hasn't been too easy lately with Bill still out every day looking for work. I was just getting myself and the kids ready to leave. I need some things at the grocery store."

"That's okay, I can stay here and watch the little ones until you get back."

"That would be great, but I can't afford to pay you much for baby-sitting."

Tracy took off her coat. "I don't want any money. I like spending time with your kids."

Mrs. Anderson smiled gratefully. "I don't know what to say. You've helped out so much lately. I know that when I see your mother I'll tell her how wonderful you've been toward our family. That's hardly a reward, but it's about the best I can do right now."

"You don't have to say anything to her about this, Mrs. Anderson. Just helping has been its own reward."

Christianity isn't obsessed with receiving public praise. It isn't preoccupied with selfish interests such as getting extra money or votes.

What Christianity is indeed is the good news of a man named Jesus, who took upon Himself the sins of the world almost 2,000 years ago. It is also knowing that while we are deserving of eternal damnation, we are instead considered blameless before God because of Christ's death. But the Christian faith does not stop there. It is also the story of Christians sharing Christ's love with others. They let their families, communities, and planet see the effect their Lord's love has on them. They share it in ways that are often unnoticed by the public, sometimes difficult to accomplish, but always motivated by Christ's love working in them.

Prayer: How Do You Get It to Work?

God is not a cosmic bellboy for whom we can press a button to get things.

— *Harry Emerson Fosdick*

As the two boys trudged to Jefferson School, eight-year-old Marcus remarked, "I sure wish I had a pony to ride to school. Walking four blocks each way every day is killing my feet."

"Have you tried praying for one?" asked Larry.

"Naw, last week I asked God for a motorcycle and the week before that a spaceship. He didn't listen to me then, so I doubt if He'll start now."

Real love includes concern for the ultimate well-being of the one being loved. Such love doesn't necessarily show itself in giving a person everything that is requested. A mother and father, for example, may choose not to give their child a new 10-speed bike when one is requested. This doesn't mean they don't love their child. Their concern for the ultimate well-being of their youngster may lead to the denial of the bike. Love shows itself in doing what is best in the long run for the one being loved.

Similarly, God answers our prayers out of concern for our long-range good. He sees things from a perspective unattainable to us. He knows what is best for us. When we fail to receive what we pray for, it isn't an indication that God doesn't hear us or love us. Rather, it shows that He knows better than we what is best for us in the long run.

It's tempting to wish that God would grant us everything we request through prayer. But we lack both the wisdom and discipline always to know what is truly in our own best interest.

Perhaps we also need to rethink what it is we ask God for in prayer. Our prayers are often loaded with requests for things that are within our own power to achieve. It's fine to ask God for things. But it's laziness if we pray in the hope that God will do our chores for us. For instance, we should not pray for God to patch up a relationship we have with someone unless we are ready to work toward that reconciliation. In the same way, it is folly to ask God to help an acquaintance of ours who is down in the dumps unless we are ready to aid that person ourselves—with the help of God. Instead of asking Him to do our work for us, we need to ask Him to be with us as we perform our tasks.

Many times we pray that God will make our lives easier. We want God to remove problems from our lives. Maybe it would be better if instead we prayed for the strength to face our problems. God has given us abilities to meet challenges. His help in giving us the necessary courage and faith is invaluable.

Christians are not guaranteed a life of total happiness. Christianity is not insurance against misfortune. It is, though, continual trust in God's power to help us through both the good and the bad of life. So we continue to pray, assured that God will do for us what is best. We know that He has done so in the past, and we rely on His promise for the future.

Did Jesus Really Mean That?

"Lord, if my brother keeps on sinning against me, how many times do I have to forgive him? Seven times?"
"No, not seven times," answered Jesus, "but seventy times seven."
— *Matthew 18:21–22*

Most of us are familiar with Jesus' answer to Peter's question. When we first heard the story we were probably surprised that we're expected to forgive someone that often. But we shrugged it off, thinking, "Well, Jesus didn't really mean seventy times seven. He just meant we should be willing to forgive people often."

The problem is that while we might go along with what Jesus said, we are seldom willing to do what He said. We have trouble forgiving once or twice, let alone 490 times.

Suppose, for example, your friend Mary tells you during lunch hour that Angela has been telling some of the other girls about you. She's been saying that you were responsible for taking the lost pens from her locker. You know that you didn't take them and suspect that Angela is simply jealous of your popularity. You talk to her after school and she apologizes for blaming you. Do you forgive her?

Now suppose that a few days later you again hear that Angela has been talking about you. She's been making fun of the way you act in a group. You know that she's doing it so that your friends will think less of you and more of her. Do you forgive her? Do you wait to talk to her to see if she sincerely apologizes before you forgive her? Do you withhold your forgiveness if she doesn't seem very sorry for what she did?

When Jesus answered Peter's question He indicated that our love is to be limitless. We needn't be governed by the rules of justice or fairness. We needn't think that we should forgive only when the guilty party deserves our forgiveness. We can show our love independently of the other's actions.

Jesus gave His life so that all people could be forgiven. In doing so He brought about a revolution in the way people can think about forgiveness. The old "eye for an eye, tooth for a tooth" philosophy is discarded. Forgiveness no longer comes only as a result of the guilty party doing something to make up for the sin. Sins are forgiven out of love. Jesus loved us enough to come to earth, live a life of perfect obedience, and take upon Himself the punishment for our sins. The fact that we can stand forgiven before God isn't fair. We didn't receive the punishment we deserved.

Because of this we are now free to forgive each other unfairly. In other words, we can forgive others even when they don't deserve it. It's really immaterial whether the other person needs our forgiveness once, twice, or 490 times.

Despair

Joy comes, grief goes, we know not how.
— James Russell Lowell

Joel was 15 at the time of his accident. He had been a C student, had a few friends, and was interested in athletics. His inability to be more popular was a constant source of aggravation. Attempts to force others to like him met with failure.

His father had left the family when Joel was 12. Being the oldest of three children, he was expected to spend much of his time caring for his two younger sisters. It meant less time was available for Joel to spend with people his own age. For the most part, Joel was a lonely young man. And things would get worse.

One day, because of a bicycle accident, Joel lost the full use of his left leg. Although he eventually learned to walk without crutches, he had a noticeable, permanent limp. This was to cause far-reaching repercussions. Basketball and football, once sources of joy, were now virtually eliminated from Joel's life. The simple act of walking through the school hallway was an embarrassment. It was obvious that he was the object of stares. He found that people avoided him even more than before.

His problems, previously manageable, were now amplified. He began to resent the fact that his mother made him care for his two sisters. He had few enough friends at school. How could he develop any new friendships if he had to baby-sit at home all the time?

The issue of his father leaving the family now often resurfaced in Joel's mind. He began to wonder more and more if it was because of him.

And why wasn't he able to get his grades up? Why wasn't schoolwork as easy for him as it was for the others?

For quite some time things seemed to get worse. He saw himself as an unpopular, rejected, limp-legged boy. Life held little promise. The accident had been devastating.

Gradually, though, a glimmer of hope emerged. It came as the result of untold hours spent alone and in prayer. As a result of this and the passage of time, Joel was finally able to piece things together again. He was able to establish some friendships. He learned to take on new interests, and with more time spent on his studies, his grades improved a little.

He began to adjust. Little by little things worked themselves out. His sisters became more responsible as they got older and he was able to be with his friends more. He began to see that his father's leaving was beyond his control. He was able to accept that situation. Sometimes he found discouragements to be more commonplace than encouragements, but with time his outlook became more optimistic.

With life come some serious, long-lasting troubles such as those encountered by Joel. The disintegration of a relationship, the discovery that an important goal will never be reached, or the death of someone close are other examples. Events such as these can be far more than mere disappointments. They carry with them the threat of devastation.

When profound setbacks occur we may feel rejected or become despondent. We might think that life can't get any worse. Yet we're afraid that it will. It is at such times of despair that we may begin to question the reason for our existence and wonder if life is even worth living, as Joel did.

Feelings of despair do not indicate the loss of one's sense of reason. They are not signs of mental or emotional sickness. They are simply feelings that humans have at some points in their lives.

In fact, a feeling of helplessness is a necessary step toward a new beginning. It is in times of despondence that a person lets go of vain hopes and superficial dreams and sees life in its reality. A person is enabled to see through the transparency of passing pleasures. One is able to get a more accurate picture of life's meaning. The meaningless fluff of life is stripped away.

It is in a state of utter helplessness that a human can see the need for God's love in Christ. A person simply can't make it alone. The need for Christ's help becomes more obvious. Only when thoughts of self-sufficiency are shoved aside can room be made for God to fill the void. In Joel's case, improvement began when he quit trying to make it completely on his own. He put his trust in the Lord. This helped him to establish new priorities.

Despair is frightening. It is a feeling of desolation. But it begins a person on a necessary path. When one can see his inadequacy and sinfulness, one can then experience the joy of God's acceptance. One can hear God say yes to every no of the world. As Jesus once died and rose, so we are drawn close to the grave by our despair and later allowed to breathe the fresh air of new life.

The poet Carl Sandburg once wrote, "Life is like an onion: you peel it off one layer at a time and sometimes you weep." Life is certainly not a never-ending state of happiness. Even the joy which comes from the Lord is tempered by problems. But what gives us the joy is knowing that our ultimate destiny is one of total fulfillment in Christ.

Trying to Figure God Out

The created world is but a parenthesis in eternity.
— *Thomas Browne*

A teacher was explaining to her fourth-graders that the law of gravity keeps objects on the ground. A curious student interrupted, "But what kept things sticking to earth before the law was passed?"

Concepts such as the ones involving the physical laws of nature are troubling to people. How or when they began is even more confusing. To speak about the beginning of things, we are drawn into thinking about the beginning of God. But we know that God has always existed. He had no beginning. If He had a beginning He wouldn't be God. The human mind just can't conceive of an existence without a beginning. Everything we see—trees, buildings, people, even the earth itself, began at some point. God didn't.

A person's brain weighs only about three or four pounds. It is limited in what it can comprehend. When a person tries to understand the mysteries of God Himself, the brain's limitations become all too obvious. We try to picture God in terms with which we are familiar. But in drawing these pictures we so distort things that the resulting image is hardly even close to reality. When we try to give questions about God's characteristics neatly defined answers, the result is a muddled-up distortion of what He really is. God's being defies categorization in human terms.

For example, we speak of God as being eternal which, of course, He is. But in trying to understand how God can be eternal, we say He has no beginning and no ending. That also is true. But in thinking in this manner we inevitably think in terms of time. We try to put God on a time line. He doesn't belong there. People fit neatly onto time lines, but God does not. He is above the concept of time. Time was created for people and things that have a measurable duration on earth. God does not. He is not subject to time. He is the Creator of it. Eternity is not an endless time line. Eternity exists above and outside the concept of time.

People similarly falter when they try to ascribe physical characteristics to God. Traditionally we have pictured God as an elderly, white-haired gentleman looking down at us from above. We see Him as having an all-knowing look on His face. But God isn't limited to a particular form or appearance. He has no face or body. He doesn't live within the confines of a bordered area. He is beyond that realm. God isn't someone that can be included as part of a picture in which He poses with other people. He is the artist of the picture.

Well, if our attempts to categorize God in human terms are so inaccurate, how can we think of Him? It does us no harm to continue to see God in the ways we formerly did. If, for example, we picture God as having eyes and hands that protect us from danger, that may be of comfort to us. There is nothing wrong with picturing God in human terms.

We need, though, to see that God is not subject to the same limitations as people. He doesn't get too tired or too busy or too old to help us. He is God, not simply some superhuman. We no longer need to think, "I wonder if God can . . . " He can because He is God.

Acting Concerned vs. Concerned Action

Doctor: Well, your leg is swollen, but I wouldn't worry about it.
Patient: No, and if your leg was swollen I wouldn't worry about it either.

Two women walked home from church together. Their two daughters trailed behind. The women were discussing the sermon.

"Pastor is right. There's so much suffering in the world. We need to do something. To imagine that all those people go to bed hungry each night!"

"And the people who have to live in those war-torn countries, I really feel sorry for them. I saw a piece about them on the news the other night. No home, little food, little to live for. It just made me sick."

"And things aren't so great in our own country, either. Did you see on the news how many people stood in line to fill out job applications when that electronics firm announced a few openings? I really feel sorry for them. They want to find work and just can't."

"And then there's Mrs. Marten. First her husband passed away last month and now Pastor announces that she's been sick lately also."

"You know, Ethel, there must be something we can do for some of those people. We're both so fortunate. There must be some way we can bend down to help those who are less fortunate. Maybe we could send a check to a charity or something."

"You're right. We'll have to remember to do that." Ethel walked into her house as Catherine continued on to her own house. Their two teenage daughters were still a few blocks behind. They had decided to stop and visit Mrs. Marten.

They listened as the elderly woman talked about how hard it had been for her lately. They told her about things they'd been doing in school. She seemed interested in them and they were interested in her. The girls were on their way out when they noticed the dishes piled up in the kitchen sink. Even though Mrs. Marten said that she would eventually get to them, they knew it would be easier for them to do. After the last dish was dried they told the lady they'd be back the next day. Then they hurried home.

Human suffering can be seen from different perspectives. Some people choose to stand tall and look down at the suffering of others. They see themselves as occasionally bending low to give help. They feel that any help they give is an extraordinary act, something worthy of special recognition.

Others look around and see the suffering. They become part of it in order to be of help. For them, giving help is not an extraordinary act; it is a natural one. They understand that life in Jesus is a life of servanthood. Their role is to reveal the presence of a loving God in the middle of man's hate-filled world. They know that to be a servant means to get involved. For them, words of sympathy don't replace acts of service. Thoughts of concern aren't as helpful as deeds of kindness.

Perhaps some people are turned off by words such as servanthood and self-sacrifice. They picture a Christian as one who deliberately heaps suffering on himself. The more that can be endured, the better the Christian, they think. As a result, they choose not to adopt such a life-style.

But that's a misconception. Suffering is not the goal of a Christian. Seeing how much pain one can endure is mindless. Christians realize that in helping others they may have to sacrifice their time or energy or possessions. But they also know that they receive far more than they give. A smile of appreciation is worth far more to them than what was sacrificed. It is in helping that joy is experienced. It is in sharing that one receives.

The question, then, is not how much self-sacrificing a person can tolerate. Jesus did the sacrificing. The question is how we can make Jesus' action evident to others through our lives. It's not a burdensome sacrifice for us. It's a privilege.

Sitting Alone in the School Cafeteria

No man is an island, entire of itself.

— *John Donne*

Picture a group of boys at a summer camp. They go out into a woods together, looking for the required items for a scavenger hunt. After a while one of the boys, Tom, realizes that he has become separated from the others. He wanders through the woods, hoping to spot the group.

Tom would like to call out for help, but he decides to keep quiet. His shouting might be interpreted by the rest of the boys as a sign of being afraid. So he keeps walking in silence, anxiously hoping to be reunited with the rest of the group.

After a few nervous hours Tom finds his way back to the camp. It is then that he learns that each of the boys in the group had become separated from the others. All of them had been walking, looking for each other. All had chosen to be silent for fear of being ridiculed by the others. Each had thought that he was the only one lost, the only one not part of the group. In searching for each other their paths had often crossed. But with each one staying quiet, none of them knew how close they had been to spotting the other. Therefore, they had stayed separated much longer.

Now picture a group of high school freshmen. They are beginning their journey through the high school years, each hoping to find the things that will be required of them later in life. One of the boys, Kevin, soon feels separated from his classmates. He keeps to himself, not saying much for fear of being ridiculed if he says or does something wrong. He walks to class by himself, feels isolated from the others in the classroom, and eats alone in the school cafeteria. He is anxious to find a friend or two, but he is too shy to assert himself and make any friends.

Eventually Kevin finds a few friends, and as time goes on his list of friends grows quite large. It is then that he realizes how wrong he had been when he first started high school. He thought that he was the only one who felt lonely, the only one isolated from the group. He thought that everyone else had plenty of friends and that they were all charter members of "the group." But now he sees that the others experienced the same feeling of isolation and rejection. Each was looking for what Kevin would have gladly given them—friendship. Each, in turn, would have gladly given Kevin friendship had they only known of his needs.

While some people feel a greater need to belong to a group than others, everyone needs friends. Individuals require the companionship of others. Each needs the giving and receiving of a relationship with other people.

The problem is that it can be difficult for a person to make friends when placed in an environment such as a new high school or college. Young people in particular may be uncertain of what strategies to employ in reaching out to someone else. As was the case with both Tom and Kevin, the fear of ridicule makes some people keep quiet. It may be easier to keep to oneself than to be assertive and risk rejection.

Perhaps it is helpful to remember that we are not the only person looking for friends. Others have the same desires. There are a lot of lonely people in the world who are looking for someone with whom to share a friendship. These people obviously don't carry a sign that reads "I Am Lonely." People usually don't want others to know this and therefore try to appear anything but lonely. They may do so in a variety of ways. They might do their best to conform to the latest fads, or bury their head inside a set of stereo headphones, or act as though they prefer to be alone even when they don't. But these disguises don't make them any less lonely.

A good way to show Christian love is to work at beginning a friendship with someone who is lonely. When attempting this, common sense strategies are best. Be generous with warm smiles, call the person by their first name, be a good listener, don't be afraid to compliment, and most important—be yourself. Don't put on an act. These approaches aren't guaranteed to work all the time. But they do help to make people feel at ease. And that's the first step.

The attempts to begin a new friendship may be initially uncomfortable. But a show of concern may well be just what that person is hoping for. The beginning of a friendship may mean the ending of loneliness for both people involved.

Life with Mother

There are only two lasting bequests we can give our children. One of these is roots; the other, wings.

— Hodding Carter

"Oh, Mom, why do you have to ask so many questions about my private life? I'm not your little girl anymore, you know!" Her mouth just seemed to blurt out the words. Janet wished she hadn't said them and yet was glad that she had.

Her mother seemed hurt by the remark and said nothing. They both sat there, silent, staring at the casserole on their plates.

While Janet's mouth stayed closed, her mind stayed busy. "Why does she have to be so nosy? She's got to let me be on my own more. Why can't she learn to trust me?"

On the other side of the table her mother too was quietly rethinking what had just happened. "All I did was ask her about what she's doing on her date this weekend. What's so wrong with that? I know she doesn't like it when I ask so many questions, it's just that I'm concerned about her. Maybe I'm overly protective, but it scares me to think that something might happen to her. I just hope she realizes that a lot of bad can happen these days."

"Pass the butter, please."

"Here."

"Thanks."

Janet poured herself another glass of milk. "I wonder if she really knows how I feel. Maybe she doesn't understand that I've got to be given more freedom without her prying around all the time."

Her mother reflected, "I wish she could understand what a mother goes through in raising a child. All the worries — it's so overwhelming. Will she be healthy? Will she be smart enough? Will she grow up to be a normal child? Will she be accepted by others? I wish she could see what a mother goes through. When I was raising her I was so pleased the way she could always tell me about how things were going for her. She'd ask for my advice and I'd be able to use my years of experience to help her. I thought it would always be that way. I guess I was wrong."

"Want more casserole?"

"No thanks, Mom."

The last few minutes of almost total silence had allowed each of them to think things through more objectively.

Janet continued to talk to herself: "I suppose it can't be very easy for Mom either. There are a lot of problems someone my age could get into. It's only natural for her to be concerned. I guess it's a good thing she is. I just wish she would give me more freedom, at least a little more. I'm not so sure I want too much. I guess I feel a little insecure when I'm totally on my own. I want more freedom. I know that. But I also want to know that she's there when I need her. I'm confused. Maybe the reason I sounded off to her was to convince myself that I really wanted her to stay out of things. But now I'm not sure I do."

Her mother finished eating. "Maybe I'll just have to learn to accept the fact that Janet is getting older and needs to feel that she is trusted by me," Mom thought. "I can't keep blaming her when she isn't so willing to talk and come to me for advice like she once did."

Janet was finishing her meal also. "Even if she keeps asking so many questions, I think I can accept that. I'll probably be a lot like her when I become a mother. Come to think of it, I hope I will."

"I can do the dishes myself tonight, Mom. You can take it easy."

"I'll help. They'll get done faster that way. Besides, that will give us a chance to talk."

"Okay, Mom."

Standing on the Shoulders of Giants

If I have seen further it is by standing on the shoulders of giants.
— Isaac Newton

The city's new luxury spa was now open. The man first washed himself in the hot, steamy pool. He then walked over to the warm water pool to relax and talk over the news with his old buddies. Finally, he took a refreshing dive in the cold water pool. "What a life," thought the man.

That afternoon he would stroll over to the city's sports stadium. It seated 20,000 spectators and was so well planned that all of the people could enter or exit it in under 10 minutes. When the sun got too hot a canvas roof was placed over the seating area. It wasn't exactly a domed stadium, but for a city of only 50,000, it was more than adequate.

A city of the 80s? Yes, but not the 1980s. This was a city of A.D. 80. It was a city in the Roman Empire. Cities constructed by the Romans more than 1,900 years ago were amazingly modern.

Some cities used aqueducts to supply themselves with fresh water from lakes more than 40 miles away. Others had sewer systems that worked well for hundreds of years without problems.

Many of the streets built by the Romans lasted for more than 1,000 years. Some city streets were built about 18 inches lower than the sidewalks. Designed with a crown down the middle, they channeled rainwater into the sewer lines below the sidewalks. Stepping stones were placed across streets. Using these, a pedestrian could keep his or her feet dry while crossing the temporarily wet streets. Since the stepping stones were higher than the level of the street, carts and animals using the street had to straddle them very slowly. This helped lower the noise level and increase safety. And we thought speed bumps were a recent invention!

The study of ancient cultures reveals a surprising degree of technological sophistication. It soon becomes apparent that our modern society has no monopoly on ingenuity.

It is foolish to think that we are an enlightened society or that we are in some way superior to those who lived before us. We are able to have the advances of our age because of the work of our predecessors. We need to appreciate the efforts of the thousands of people who have spent countless hours to give us what we have.

We also need to do what is possible to make the world better for future generations. Just as God gave the people of the past the ability to think and work, so He now gives it to us. The responsibilities that were at one time on our forefathers' shoulders now lie with us.

Our society's job is not to see how many more inventions can be produced. It is to feed, clothe, house, educate, and spiritually nourish the earth's inhabitants. Unless our concern is for the uplifting of people, any new technologies we develop will do little good.

Perhaps, then, as career plans are made, it would be good to first consider those occupations of direct service to people. No one person can save the world's population, but each can lay plans to do whatever is possible to show what Christ's death and resurrection now means for the people of this planet. While new scientific advances are fine, it is what each of us does for others that really matters.

Are You Mr. Right?

Love does not consist in gazing at each other but in looking outward together in the same direction.
— Antoine de Saint-Exupéry

When a girl meets a guy, she subconsciously begins to categorize him. Is he cute? Does he have a sense of humor? Is he intelligent? Is he interesting? Is he in the same league as me? Is he already taken? If the boy meets the girl's standards, she will probably continue her interest in him. Meanwhile, he is subjecting her to the same kinds of questions. Usually the relationship never gets off the ground. One or both of the people have insufficient interest in the other.

But once in a while a relationship does begin. The two people are attracted to each other and begin to spend time together. As time goes on, the relationship may continue to develop. At some point, the word *love* might begin to be used. The two acquire a special feeling for each other.

There's an old saying that love is blind. When two people feel strongly about each other, they may overlook the faults their companions have. Ben Franklin once wrote, "If Jack's in love, he's no judge of Jill's beauty." By this he was referring to the way love can blind a person to everything but the good of the other.

It's common for a person to begin idolizing his or her companion shortly after they begin a relationship. Everything that this boyfriend or girlfriend does is right. Sometimes undesirable traits in a companion are tolerated when those same characteristics would never be tolerated in someone else.

High school has a way of making some people feel they're under pressure to find a steady. If they're not going with someone, there must be something wrong with them. That, of course, is nonsense. But it's believed by enough people to make some rush into a relationship simply in order to comply with the expectations of the group.

Such logic hardly makes for a strong or lasting relationship. It's important to view a boyfriend or girlfriend objectively and to be honest about differences. There's far more to a lasting relationship than mutual physical attraction or the ability to have a good time together for a few hours.

Questions about the strength of a relationship can be answered only after much time has passed. The two people need to experience many different kinds of situations together. How do they react to adversity? How well can the two get along when they're doing something boring together? What happens when they move past the idolizing stage and see their friend's faults? How well do they take criticism from each other? Do they have similar goals in life? Do they share their faith in Christ?

There's a joke about a young man named Jim and his friend. It illustrates what can happen as a result of rushing to find a companion.

Jim's friend asked, "Why do you go steady with Lucy?"

"She's different from the other girls," was Jim's reply.
"How is she different?"
"She's the only girl who will go with me."

The pressure of high school can bring two people together who may not have much in common. There's no need to be in a hurry to find a life's companion. The test of time gives a more accurate indication of the strength of a relationship than the feelings brought on by the pressure of schoolmates. People need time to sort things out. Major decisions such as choosing a life's partner need to be made only after much time is spent in thought and prayer.

Worship That's Worth It

The most exalted privilege in life is to have intimate daily, hourly fellowship with God.

— A. P. Gouthey

Domitian was the emperor of Rome during the closing years of the first century, about 50 years after Jesus' ascension. Few Roman rulers have been so arrogant. He took over the absolute rule of the empire by compelling the Roman Senate to vote as he wished. His desire to be revered as the supreme head of the empire led him to act in strange ways.

Men were made to fall to their hands and knees and kiss Domitian's hands or feet when they met him. He invited guests to evening receptions. These guests were then expected to take turns praising him. Domitian would sit in silence, listening to the accolades but seldom responding.

Such actions led to public hatred of the emperor. After some unsuccessful attempts, he was finally killed with the help of his wife. His death was followed by public rejoicing.

Throughout the ages people have praised and worshiped their rulers in various ways. But such reverence seldom took such an extreme form as it did for Domitian. Even today people publicly display their respect for rulers. Generally, the more important the public office, the greater the honor paid.

This raises the question about what form of praise is appropriate for God, the ultimate Ruler. Certainly He deserves far more adoration than any earthly ruler. But what is a fitting way to show reverence for Him, for instance, in a church service?

The answer lies in the fact that God, unlike earthly rulers, has no ego to be fed. He isn't impressed with the chatter of worshipers as they mindlessly repeat words or actions of praise. God doesn't need His people to offer up words of worship just to make Him feel good.

A church service best serves God when the worshipers are brought closer to Him through songs, words, and thoughts. In this process, people don't so much communicate with God; God communicates with people. The result is a oneness with Him. Worship of earthly kings illustrates the separation between the common people and the king. Meaningful worship of God shows the unity of God and all His people.

The End?

One short sleep past, we wake eternally,
And death shall be no more;
Death, thou shalt die.

— *John Donne*

His eyes opened. He searched for the bedside clock. It was six a.m. Another day was upon him. He stared at the walls of his bedroom. He had helped build those same walls more than 50 years before. He was young then, in his middle 20s. He was strong too. Now he was neither. His eyes fixed upon the picture next to the dresser. It was taken years ago when he and his wife were vacationing. Those were happier years. Now he was alone. He had buried Margaret back in 1975.

When he was younger he had so little free time. His work and family responsibilities seemed to take up his whole day. He seldom was able to take life easy back then. Now he had time, plenty of it. But now there seemed to be little to enjoy.

He reached for his cane and walked to the kitchen to make himself a cup of coffee. There was little on his schedule for the day. He'd read a little, watch some television, eat, nap, and walk to the store. That would be it. Tomorrow he'd do the same. There wasn't much he wanted to do these days, nor was there much he could do. An operation the year before had restricted his activity. He was happy to have had it, though. It had saved his life. He wasn't especially happy with life, but he knew he didn't want to die.

There are millions of people like him in the world today. They seemingly have little to live for, but they don't want to die either. Death is their enemy. It's something to be avoided at all cost. The discomfort of life on earth is preferable to the threat of what death will bring.

But for Christians death isn't the ultimate adversary. It serves definite functions, each of which is of value to the Christian. First, it brings to mind the meaning of life. It reminds us of the time limits imposed upon us. It makes each day and what to do with that day more significant. It emphasizes to us that there is so much to do on this earth and so little time in which to do it.

Secondly, it provides a permanent end to people's suffering. Pain, trouble, and worry are ended with death. They don't reappear. Wouldn't it be tragic if we couldn't die? Wouldn't it be more terrible if people stayed alive indefinitely? Old, weary, painful bodies would continue to stay alive. Yet they would be unable to find relief from themselves. Paul's statement in Philippians 3:20–21 can be of comfort to those whose bodies are no longer strong and healthy. "We eagerly wait for our Savior, the Lord Jesus Christ, to come from heaven. He will change our weak mortal bodies and make them like His own glorious body, using that power by which He is able to bring all things under His rule."

Lastly, death brings with it a blessing. With death comes the arrival of heaven—forever. Our journey through life, trusting in Christ as we go, is then complete. Life can be agonizing at times, but it is a road to something far better.

Death, then, is a step toward greater things. Christians live in faith and die in faith. We are Christ's children on both sides of the grave.

For I am certain that nothing can separate us from His love: neither death nor life, neither angels nor other heavenly rulers or powers, neither the present nor the future, neither the world above nor the world below—

there is nothing in all creation that will ever be able to separate us from the love of God which is ours through Christ Jesus our Lord.
—Romans 8:38 –39

Living in the Fast Lane

*There was a young lady named Bright,
Whose speed was far faster than light;
She set out one day
In a relative way,
And returned home the previous night.*

— Arthur Buller

We live in a fast-moving world. Computers calculate difficult problems in milliseconds. Package delivery services promise overnight delivery. Cars race around a track at 200 miles per hour.

A man once jumped into a taxi and shouted to the driver, "Step on it!" The cabby raced the car down the street, dodging everything in his way. Within a few minutes the cab was speeding along the expressway. After some time it dawned on the passenger that he hadn't told the driver his destination. He yelled to the cabby, "Hey, buddy, did I tell you where I wanted to go?"

"No, but I'm going as fast as I can," was the reply.

It's easy to get caught up in the frantic pace of society. We hurry to get into a waiting line. We hurry to get to our next class before the bell rings. We hurry to get to the store before it closes.

It's important to be prompt. But maybe by rushing so much we're missing out on a lot also. Maybe we're taking too many shortcuts. For instance, pretend you're on your way home from school to watch a television program. You see your elderly neighbor outside. She'd probably like it if you would stop to talk to her for a few minutes. She'd like some company. You really don't want to take the time. You want to watch your program. What do you do? It's safe to assume that the conversation would mean more to your neighbor than the television program would to you.

God's purpose for us isn't to see how quickly we can do things. It's to have us be of help to each other. When we see that all of our hurrying is getting in the way of that, we need to slow down.

It's important to decrease our pace at times and see things from a slow-motion perspective. Seeing that God is in control of us and that we are in control of our lives because of this is vital. "Be still and know that I am God" (Psalm 46:10 NIV) was timely advice when it was written long ago. It's just as timely in the age of the computer.

The Sadness of Beauty

*To see a world in a grain of sand,
And a heaven in a wild flower,
Hold infinity in the palm of your hand,
And eternity in an hour.*

— William Blake

The two walked hand in hand along the sands. Thoughts of his business responsibilities and her office work were behind them now. Their vacation had begun. The waves pounded in, thundering, but not evoking fear. Seagulls were but specks against the reddish sky. The sun, which would soon disappear for another night, was sharing one last burst of brilliance.

"Isn't it beautiful, Jeff?" Julie mused. She was struck by the beauty of the sunset. This was a moment in which time itself seemed to stand still. The moment was one of unspeakable beauty, a celebration of life.

Yet Julie wasn't smiling. In fact, a hint of sadness was on her face. Her joy was bridled by the realities of the world. The sun would soon set. The sky would darken. The vacation would eventually end. Life in the office would begin again.

Julie's reaction was a common one. The enjoyment of beauty is never very long lasting. It is always tempered by the ugliness of the "real" world, the sin-filled world we have built for ourselves.

But beauty does more than give us a moment's distraction from the reality of life on this earth. It points us to a greater good. It shows us that above the frustrations of the world is a divine plan. The beauty of a sunset or a flower or a bird's song reminds us of the artistic hand of God. Beyond the disappointments of everyday life stands a God who cares. He shows us glimpses of perfection and of what is to come. Scenic mountains and meticulously fashioned snowflakes indicate His design of beauty in nature.

But His master design is shown not just in nature. God's foremost creation, His people, also manifests His goodness. Living friends, warm smiles, and thoughtful words all reflect the Lord's love for us. Sinful as we are, God uses us to bear witness to His care. We receive His blessings through the words and actions of others. And likewise, we share this fortune with others.

The greatest hint of God's concern for us is one that we can't see. It's revealed to us in His Word. The fact that almost 2,000 years ago Jesus, God's Son, took upon Himself the suffering for our sins is the ultimate proof of a loving God. And it is because of this fact that life can take on meaning for us.

Plenty of things go wrong in this world. At times it seems there's hardly room for the beauty of creation to make more than a short appearance; yet the goodness of life isn't just a fleeting moment's pleasure. It is the foundation upon which God's creation began and continues to exist. The love of God stands eternal.

Burying the Hatchet vs. Bearing the Hatchet

With malice toward none; with charity for all; ... let us strive on to finish the work we are in.

— Abraham Lincoln

Henry Ward Beecher once said, "Those who say 'I can forgive, but I cannot forget' are really saying 'I cannot forgive.' " Truly forgiving someone sounds easy, but it is very difficult. There have been some remarkable examples of forgiveness in recorded history. Here is one:

When Abraham Lincoln became president in 1861, 11 Southern states decided to leave the Union. They did this chiefly because of differences with the North regarding slavery. The North felt it was necessary to prevent the South from separating itself from the Union. So the Civil War began.

Lincoln spent his first presidential term doing what he could to end the strife as quickly as possible. The responsibilities placed upon him were enormous, and they took their toll. He aged much in those four years, and his life was complicated immensely by the struggle.

By the end of his first term the Civil War was still going on, and Lincoln had taken much criticism for his handling of the war. Yet he managed to win reelection, and on March 4, 1865, he gave a speech at his second inauguration as President of the United States. As he stood in front of the Capitol that day, his words were not bitter words. He did not try to revenge the angry criticism hurled at him. Nor did he try to deflect the blame. His words stressed the importance of forgetting about past animosities. He wanted the war to end and for the two sides to again become one nation. He spoke about the reasons for the war and the importance of trust in the providence of God. He ended his speech with these words:

Fondly do we hope—fervently do we pray—that this mighty scourge of war may speedily pass away.... With malice toward none; with charity for all, with firmness in the right as God gives us to see the right, let us strive on to finish the work we are in; to bind up the nations's wounds; to care for him who shall have borne the battle, and for his widow, and his orphan—to do all which may achieve and cherish a just and lasting peace, among ourselves and with all nations.

Altogether the Civil War left more than 600,000 soldiers dead and another half million wounded. It devastated both farmland and cities; it split the country apart like nothing had before. Hatred abounded. Yet Lincoln spoke about binding up the nation's wounds, about leaving the past behind and making a new beginning.

But he did more than simply speak about unity. As the war's end finally appeared within sight, Lincoln established policies regarding what would happen when it ended. Many people in the North disliked what Lincoln had decided. They wanted the South to be punished. But Lincoln wasn't concerned with punishment. He wanted the healing to begin.

General Lee of the South surrendered his army to General Grant on April 9, 1865. But some fighting was still going on in other areas. On April 14 Lincoln was shot. He died the next morning, never seeing the peace and healing he had worked throughout his presidency to achieve.

Abraham Lincoln is often cited as an example of a great American leader. Sometimes people seem to give him almost godlike reverence. This, of course, is inappropriate. Lincoln was far from perfect. Perhaps he has been given more credit by some than he deserves. But his ability to forgive can be instructive.

Lincoln was willing to forgive the past and to get on with the process of oneness. He did this in spite of all the personal blame he had taken. The war had ruined his presidency. If he could both speak and act in such a manner, it seems that it should be comparatively easy for us to forgive. Few, if any, of the injustices done to us can approach the level experienced by Lincoln.

Because of the forgiveness we receive through Jesus' death for our sins, we are enabled to forgive others. He gives us the chance and the ability to forgive. We need to take advantage of that. By so doing we help to bring a bit more peace and friendship to our world. It's one way we can begin to thank Him for the gift we can never repay.

Another World

The earth provides enough for everyone's need, but not for everyone's greed.

— Gandhi

"What our church needs is a new lighting system—something a little fancier than we have now. The old lights have been up there for at least 20 years. I know they work all right, but I think new ones would be a nice change. Getting all new lighting and wiring would cost us a few thousand dollars, but we've got enough money in the church treasury." Mr. Jennings sat down. The chairman of the voters' meeting asked if there was any more discussion on the issue.

On the other side of the world, six-year-old Rahid searches the village for food to feed himself and his mother. He has run out of places to look. Another year of near-famine has left much of the village either dead or hopeless. The only signs of energy and health seem to come from the flies.

Another member present at the meeting stood up and asked whether the money couldn't go toward something more useful than lights. "What do you mean, more useful?" was Mr. Jennings' reply. "We need those lights. Besides, we've got to take care of ourselves. We've got to do whatever's best for our church. Why, just last month I visited St. Mark's in Uniontown. They've just installed new carpeting for the entire main floor of the church. They've really got a nice looking little church over there. And they've got fewer members than us. If they can do it, so can we. We can't let these small churches show us up, can we? Besides, the money isn't doing any good just sitting in the bank. What else could we do with the money anyway?"

Rahid's mother ground a small amount of wheat flour. It wasn't enough to fill her and Rahid, her only surviving son. But it was enough to keep them alive for a few more days. At this point, that was all they could hope for, enough to keep them going.

Matthew 25: 34 – 40 records the words of Jesus as He spoke of the responsibility His followers have in caring for those in need. It illustrates how kindness for all people, motivated by faith in Christ, is linked to kindness for the Lord Himself:

Then the King will say to the people on His right, "Come, you that are blessed by My Father! Come and possess the kingdom which has been prepared for you ever since the creation of the world. I was hungry and you fed Me, thirsty and you gave Me a drink; I was a stranger and you received Me in your homes, naked and you clothed Me; I was sick and you took care of Me, in prison and you visited Me."

The righteous will then answer Him, "When, Lord, did we ever see You hungry and feed You, or thirsty and give You a drink? When did we ever see You a stranger and welcome You in our homes, or naked and clothe You? When did we ever see You sick or in prison, and visit You?"

The King will reply, "I tell you, whenever you did this for one of the least important of these brothers of Mine, you did it for Me!"

For Better or for Worse

Teenage girl: "Do you think it's proper for a young lady to go out with a perfect stranger?"
Confused Counselor: "I think it's very difficult to even find a stranger who is perfect."

Dan and Cheryl have been married for five years now. He is a carpenter. She is a teacher. While they're quite happily married now, it wasn't always that way.

In high school, Dan was on the football team. He was popular and had a reputation as a guy who knew how to have a good time. He got into trouble at school once in a while, but he wasn't a bad guy. He just enjoyed a good laugh.

Cheryl was quiet. She was a good student and had plans to become a teacher. She planned to go to a distant city for her college education. She was more serious and self-disciplined than he.

They began going together their senior year in high school. Dan thought it would be good for his image to go out with a nice, quiet, intelligent girl like Cheryl. She could give him the stability he didn't have. Cheryl was attracted to Dan because he was fun to be around. The thought of going with a big, popular, fun-loving guy like Dan was alluring.

The two hit it off well right from the start. Soon they were seen together often. They continued to date through much of the summer after their graduation.

The problems began when Dan realized that Cheryl was serious about going off to college. All along he assumed she would change her mind and stay. That way things could continue as they had before. Dan would attend a local junior college and Cheryl could find a job and earn money. In a few years they could be married. Dan would have a job of his own by then, and Cheryl could become a housewife.

Cheryl's resolve to go off to college turned all of Dan's plans upsidedown. Dan had trouble accepting Cheryl's decision. Things either had to be done as he had planned or not at all. They broke up. Both went their separate ways.

Each made friends at their new schools and got involved in the life-style of college. But neither forgot the other. Two summers later they met by chance at a party. They began to date again and soon they were going out regularly. Slowly Dan began to respect Cheryl's wish to become a teacher, and he was not resentful when September came and Cheryl went back to school for her junior year. They promised to keep in touch, and they kept their word.

After graduating, Cheryl became a teacher at a local elementary school. By now Dan was working with a construction company. They were able to share much time together. Two years later they were married.

There was a lot of adjusting for Dan and Cheryl to do, especially after the novelty of married life first wore off. Many of the adjustments didn't come easily. Some didn't come at all. Both at one time or another thought they had made the wrong decision. Whether or not they'd stay together for a lifetime was questionable.

At first, each wanted the other to conform to their own set of expectations. Each was intolerant of the habits of the other. This led to disappointments and arguments.

The turning point came when they began to allow each other the freedom to become themselves, to pursue their own goals rather than to be molded by the other. After a while, they discovered that love gives freedom, not restrictions based on self-interest. It was by granting the other the chance to grow and mature in his or her own way that Dan and Cheryl found their similarities. They were now able to share life's experiences. Each was able to function independently while still functioning within the mutual dependence of marriage.

As they look back now, Dan and Cheryl thank God for allowing them to get back together. They see their initial relationship as being exploitive. Dan realizes that his original idea was to use Cheryl for his own purposes. He expected her to give up her dreams of a teaching career and be what he wanted her to be. He understands now how selfish he had been.

Cheryl is also able to see how she had tried to use Dan. In the beginning, deciding to go with him was based partly on her desire to be more popular at school. Once married, her intolerance of Dan's habits hurt their relationship. Cheryl's constant nagging was an attempt to prove to herself as well as to Dan that the problems of their marriage were caused by him, not her.

Each had to learn that a relationship based on selfish motives doesn't work. A lot of giving by both partners is necessary. Dan and Cheryl have learned a lot since those early years. Both are smart enough now to know that there's still much more to learn. Marriage takes practice. They know they'll have to keep working at it. They're looking forward to living and growing together.

Digging into the Past

Sow an act, and you reap a habit. Sow a habit, and you reap a character. Sow a character, and you reap a destiny.

— Charles Rea

Big city skyscrapers are colossal structures that nearly defy description. Looking up from street level at the immensity of one can be dizzying. Yet it is what one finds below the street that makes what towers above possible.

Construction of a typical skyscraper begins with the removal of surface dirt and gravel. This excavation is necessary because the dirt and gravel don't give sufficient support to things built upon them. The clay below is firmer and is less likely to give way. However, even the clay can't be trusted to bear the millions of pounds of weight of the huge building.

To support this awesome load, builders rely on the bedrock far below. In some places this bedrock is 200 feet under the surface. Much time and expense is required to transmit the weight of the building to this bedrock. Structures called bearing piles are used. These long poles are made of concrete or steel and extend down to the bedrock. Only after these bearing piles are in place can the construction of the building begin. The main supports of the skyscraper are built on top of these bearing poles so that the building will not sink or topple.

Like buildings, people are built upon foundations. Rather than concrete or steel, human experiences are what make up each person's undergirding. What we are today is the product of the influences of the past upon us. The people, schools, books, and games we have been exposed to when younger all helped to mold us.

While we have some choice in what will influence us in the future, we can't change what we have already experienced. And it's the past that so profoundly influences us in the present. The past is gone; yet it still strongly affects our present life. The past has left its indelible mark on each of us.

The construction of a huge building doesn't just happen overnight. It takes time. People too take time to develop. God used different kinds of experiences to instruct us. Some of this instruction is painful. Disappointments can be tough to take. Loneliness can be devastating. Sadness can be heartbreaking. But from these negatives can come positive results. They can teach things that good experiences alone cannot. They are part of the foundation that gives us the strength to stand upright.

Seeing God's hand in our past can help us get a clearer view of our present. We can see God's continuing care. We can realize that there are reasons for setbacks. We are also better able to put our successes in perspective. We can live in the knowledge that our good fortune is due to God, not to our own abilities or cleverness.

The future will bring with it many challenges. It's been said that experience is a hard teacher; it gives the test first and the lesson afterward. Inevitably, each of us will have to learn some lessons the hard way. People make mistakes. Perceptive people learn from their mistakes. They use the experience to grow in maturity.

Life is a matter of learning from each of our encounters. We learn from the wins, the losses, the joys, the sorrows, the brilliance, and the stupidity of our past. As we grow, we can see glimpses of God working in all of these experiences to build our foundation for the future. Whatever we are today is the result of His working in our past to prepare us for life with Him in the days and years to come.

Having Solitude as a Companion

I was never less alone than while by myself.
— Edward Gibbon

Her high school graduation was just a few days away. It had been a busy spring for Sophie. The school activities were finally winding down, and soon high school would be a thing of the past for her. She sat in her room, thinking back over the last four years. They had been good years. She had learned a lot about math and English and science and herself. It was that last subject, herself, that had taken her the longest to understand.

She reminisced about her first year in high school. She had been worried about how difficult the schoolwork would be. It hadn't taken her too long to realize that if she studied hard, the grades would take care of themselves. She also recalled her concern about having some friends. She hadn't known many people when she started there. But that too had taken care of itself. She was fortunate to have found some good friends.

When her sophomore year began, Sophie decided that the toughest year was behind her. She could now "spread her wings" and try some new things. She went to most of the games, dances, and parties. She was on the staff of the school paper and in student government. Her popularity increased, and she loved the life she was leading. At least she thought she did at the time.

Sophie continued to do the same kind of things as her junior year began. She found herself right in the middle of the mainstream. She liked being there. She also needed to be there.

But by late winter a gradual change took place. She began to realize why she felt such a need to go along with what the others were doing. It was because she felt insecure. She wasn't yet sure of herself. Having a lot of friends seemed the best way to cope with her self-doubt. Since she felt inadequate in dealing with some of life's problems, she had thought that going along with all the others was the safest thing to do.

After realizing what she had been doing, she knew it was time to make some decisions. She began to come to grips with the kinds of questions her classmates were putting off until later. With the help of her family, she started making plans for her career; she thought about what college would be best for her. While some of her friends were on paths that would lead to early marriage, Sophie decided to put off a relationship that would get in the way of her education. Her decisions were not easy to make. But she felt good about having made them.

From that point on Sophie saw herself differently. She felt more confident about herself. She became more self-assured. She was less swayed by what her friends wanted her to do. She saw that the Lord was with her. She trusted Him.

She began to realize that she didn't have to spend so much of her time with her friends. She didn't need that false sense of security anymore. She spent more time alone. She began to get in touch with her feelings—not the crowd's feelings—but hers. She was alone more, but not at all lonely. She was still involved in many extracurricular school activities. But she was involved now because she wanted to be, not because she needed to be.

She still prized her friendships. In fact, she found that it was in solitude that greater friendships develop. She was able to gain a new perspective by spending more time by herself. It gave her a vision not readily available to those who can't remove themselves from the hurry and shouting of the crowd. She could now more clearly understand her friends and their actions. She could appreciate that they too were trying as best they could to cope with the same kinds of problems that confronted her.

Her senior year was now ending. It had gone by quickly. Ever since she began to see her friendships and herself in a different light, things had changed. She was better able to deal with the problems that arose. Her self-confidence, based on her faith in God, had allowed things to flow more smoothly for her.

College would bring with it new challenges. Sophie knew she would encounter problems she hadn't even considered. But as she sat in her room with graduation just around the corner, she felt good about the future.

A Case Study of Two Doctors

The happiest men are those who are thankful for life's responsibilities, not for its prizes.

— Gloria Pitzer

Once upon a time there were two doctors. One began his medical practice in a big city. The other started in a small rural town. The big-city doctor specialized in neurological disorders. The other was a general practitioner.

The big-city doctor worked at a large hospital. He had regular, scheduled hours. Wednesday was his day off. He usually played golf. The other worked in a small office. Since he was the only doctor in town, he was called upon day and night, whenever someone needed him. He had no days off, although he tried to keep away from his work on Sunday.

Both doctors were good at what they did. The big-city doctor was paid handsomely for his time. Skills like his were rare, even in such a large city. The small-town doctor didn't charge much. Sometimes he didn't charge anything if the patient couldn't afford to pay.

After some years the big-city doctor moved on to a new hospital in another large city. He was paid even better there. His new location was also more convenient for him to conduct lectures across the country regarding new medical procedures. The other doctor was still practicing in the same small town. He had offers for employment in other towns, but he turned them down. He knew that he was providing a necessary service where he was, and he was happy there. It gave him many opportunities to reflect the love he was given in Christ to those who needed help in his town.

After more time had passed, the big-city doctor became upset. He was still not offered the position as head of his department. He left to go to another hospital. He went where his efforts were better appreciated. He received many awards, and his fame as a lecturer grew. By this time the small-town doctor was delivering the babies of parents who themselves had been delivered by him years before.

Still more time passed. The big-city doctor was named head of the neurology department of a prestigious university hospital. The other continued in his same role. The years and the responsibilities had taken their toll on him. He wasn't in the best of health anymore, but he kept treating those that needed his help. He couldn't very well leave even if he wanted. Too many people relied on him.

The two doctors approached their retirement years. The big-city doctor turned to writing books on medicine. That, he thought, might give him the acclaim he deserved. The other doctor was pleased to see a new, younger doctor come to town. She took much of the burden off the shoulders of the old doctor. But still the old doctor continued to help out when needed. He liked doing that.

Both men died. The small-town doctor's life had been a success. It had been a life of trust in God's love through Christ and a commitment to share that love with the people who needed him.

Getting Around the Law

Man is the only animal that blushes. Or needs to.
— Mark Twain

A woman once fell and broke her leg. The doctor put it in a cast and told the woman not to walk up or down stairs. After three months the doctor said that it was time to remove the cast. He also said that if the leg was healed she could again climb stairs. "Good," said the woman, "I'm tired of climbing up and down the drainpipe."

The doctor had ordered the woman not to climb stairs for her own good. He wanted the leg to have a chance to heal. By doing what she did, the woman only hurt her leg. She may not have disobeyed the doctor's orders word for word. She did, however, disobey the intent, and the result was further injury.

We often do similar things. We think that by not doing exactly what a law forbids, we can skirt around it. For instance, suppose a student wants to get a good grade on a test for which he hasn't prepared. He knows the rules: no copying of answers from another student is permitted. He also knows that he can see the answers of the student sitting next to him. He decides that he'll put down answers similar to those of his neighbor, but he won't copy them word for word. That way, he thinks, he's not guilty of copying.

The student is, of course, still guilty. He has attempted to persuade himself that he hasn't disobeyed the rule. But that doesn't make him any less guilty. When we try to work our way around rules or provide excuses for our disobedience, we only hurt ourselves. It happened to the woman with the broken leg and to the student with the test, and it happens to us.

We need to "come clean" with ourselves and with God. It's absurd to think of hiding things from Him. Confession of sin begins the healing process. We admit our frailties and rely on Jesus' redeeming act to make us whole again. We can never eliminate our sinfulness. We can, though, make the best use of our abilities and trust in God's forgiveness for our failures.

The apostle John reminded his readers of this long ago. He wrote, "If we say that we have no sin, we deceive ourselves, and there is no truth in us. But if we confess our sins to God, He will keep His promises and do what is right: He will forgive us our sins and purify us from all our wrongdoing" (1 John 1:8 – 9).

When we try to hide our sins we only hurt ourselves. But when we admit our shortcomings to God, we receive the washing away of our sins by faith. What was once begun with our baptism is now relived again and again through confession.

From Here to Eternity

I expect to pass through this world but once; any good thing therefore that I can do, or any kindness that I can show to any fellow creature, let me do it now; let me not defer or neglect it, for I shall not pass this way again.

— *Stephan Grellet*

Some people say the world is a few thousand years old. Some say it's billions of years old. No one knows exactly when God created this earth. But however long ago it was, the life span of an individual is very short in comparison. Even if a person lives to be 100, it will still be only a thin slice of the total length of the earth's existence. Our time here is only a few seconds on the clock of history.

When a person is young, say 15, those 15 years seem to have lasted almost an eternity. Time seems to grind by at a painfully slow pace. But by the time a person is older, the years begin to tumble by with alarming speed. There are millions of elderly people on this earth who wonder where the years have gone.

It's easy for a young person to be lulled into thinking, "What's the hurry? I've got plenty of time. I'll help other people more in a few years, when I have more time and more money. In fact, maybe I'll even begin next summer." But things inevitably get pushed off and placed even further into the future.

Young Billy was cleaning his room one Saturday morning when he asked his mother, "Is it true that we are dust before we're born?"

His mother replied, "Well, sort of."

"And is it also true," he continued, "that we're dust after we die?"

His mother answered, "I guess so. Why?"

"Then there's somebody either coming or going under my bed."

Life on earth really is a matter of coming and going. As soon as we're born, we begin the process of dying. We begin a ride through life that will at some point stop for death.

Henry David Thoreau once said, "As if you could kill time without injuring eternity." By this, he meant that time is too precious to waste. Time that is wasted is lost forever. It's important that we use our time wisely.

God has placed us on His earth at this point in time for a reason. While we're here we are to help those who also happen to be here at this time. Our days together are few in number. Our opportunities to help are many.

The Odd Couple

Man plans, but God arranges.

— Thomas a Kempis

In the beginning he didn't even know her name. He began to notice her during his Algebra II class. She sat in the first row. He decided to strike up a conversation with her after class. They talked briefly about the assignment. After school he saw her and they talked again for a few minutes. He began to like her and she began to notice him. God looked on them and saw that it was good. Evening passed and morning came. That was the first day.

Their interest in each other began to grow as their conversations became more numerous. He liked her cute smile and pretty face.

She liked his athletic build and sense of humor. God looked on them and smiled. Evening passed and morning came. That was the second day.

He asked her out and she accepted. They went to the school's football game together. Each enjoyed the other's company. It was beginning to be a good relationship, with each one learning more about the other. They were a handsome couple. Others said they looked good together. God looked on them and continued to watch with interest. Evening passed and morning came. That was the third day.

On the following day there was no school. They didn't see each other at all. He thought about her a lot that day. He wanted the relationship to grow. He wanted to go out with her again, maybe even on a steady basis. She, too, thought much about him. God continued to watch. Evening passed and morning came. That was the fourth day.

The following day they talked for a while before school began. He was glad to see her. She was glad to see him. At lunchtime he ate with his friends. They mentioned a rumor they had heard: his new friend was spending some time with another guy.

After school he cornered her. "Why were you talking to him?"

"What's wrong with talking to him? He's a friend of mine," she answered.

"I thought I was your friend," he challenged.

"You are — or at least you were. You don't own me, you know."

Words shot back and forth like arrows. After a few minutes they parted company. Each blamed the other for the argument. God looked on them and began to wonder. Evening passed and morning came. That was the fifth day.

The next day began with both of them sure they were right. Each was determined to wait for the other to admit the mistake. Each was too stubborn to begin the process of reconciliation. By the end of the school day he told his friends that he had broken up with her. If she wanted to act the way she did, that was fine with him. Besides, she wasn't good enough for him anyway, he said. She told her friends that she had met someone new, someone less domineering. She said that the new guy was better for her. God looked on them and shook His head. Evening passed and morning came. That was the sixth day.

She dropped her book in Algebra II as she was on her way out after class. He picked it up for her. He smiled at her and she smiled at him. They began to joke around again as they walked down the hall together. They both knew that they would never go out together again. Each had realized that his initial interest in the other was based too much on physical attraction and not enough on similar interests and mutual respect. Each had since begun to nurture new interests. But they knew they could still be friends. God looked on them and saw that it was good once again.

Mindless Guilt and Guiltless Minds

Teacher: Johnny, you'll just have to improve your penmanship. I can't read your writing.
Johnny: But if I do that, you'll be able to see how bad my spelling is.

There's a story about a man who anonymously wrote letters to 10 of the most prominent men of a city. The notes read simply, "Your past has been discovered. Escape while you can." Not even pausing to ask questions, all the men left town immediately.

Each of us carries the burden of our past sins. Our failures are many, and we are keenly aware of this. As if we needed additional reminders, there are plenty of people who are quick to inform us of our misdeeds. Friends, enemies, parents, and teachers remind us daily of what we should or shouldn't have done. As a result we feel guilty much of the time. We may even feel guilty about occasionally not feeling guilty.

If success in life was based on how good we were, each of us would be total losers. We all deserve the worst. Our sins do to us what a huge chunk of iron would do to a swimmer if tied around his waist. We seemingly have little chance to survive. God has set before us His law, and we've failed to keep it. It's that simple.

But God loves us in Christ. His love is unconditional. It isn't based on the condition that we are sinless or even that we are "pretty good." It is given freely to each of us, not because we did something to deserve it, but because of what Christ did for us.

Our goal in life should not be to become perfect. Such a goal only leads to disappointment. We can't attain happiness by becoming sinless. That is impossible to achieve and isn't the purpose of life in the first place. The purpose of our existence is to go on with our lives as forgiven children of God. It is to show to our acquaintances what Christ has done and continues to do for us. His forgiveness takes us beyond the realm of what we have been into a world filled with possibilities.

We no longer need to feel burdened by our failures. A life spent in constantly mulling over past indiscretions would be meaningless. It would reflect a lack of faith in God's forgiveness. Instead, we can spend our time discovering the ways we can show God's love in our everyday life.

It's important that we do what we can to avoid offending and hurting others. But the fact is that we'll go on sinning. That won't change. We'll still often fall prey to sin. We know, however, that we are forgiven. We needn't punish ourselves or continue to feel overburdened with guilt. That won't make God love us more than He already does. We can't very adequately share the joy of our new life in Christ if we don't feel totally forgiven. There's a life for each of us, waiting to be lived. It's a life based on what Christ has done for us. It's a life worth living and sharing.

The Clockwork Universe

All are but parts of one stupendous whole,
Whose body Nature is, and God the soul.

— Alexander Pope

Sitting back, you see hundreds of stars, with an occasional arrow pointing out special points of interest in the night sky. You observe a year's movement of the stars within a few minutes. You are in a planetarium.

The stars are projected onto the ceiling of the domed building by a projector. It looks like a giant alien insect from a horror movie. Within it are levers, mirrors, and lights, all orchestrated by a computer. These intricate pieces of machinery form images on the ceiling to imitate the brightest fixed stars, the Milky Way, the sun, the moon, each of the planets, and hundreds of other stars.

As difficult as it is to make an accurate model of the real sky, that's not all these man-made marvels can do. They can, for instance, show the movement of the moon and planets independently of the stars. Or they can show what the sky looks like from different latitudes. All this is done in a scientifically accurate manner.

It's amazing that humans can so perfectly imitate nature with the use of these intricate machines. How much more amazing it is, though, that God can create and keep the real thing going. Millions of stars and heavenly bodies are continually in motion. All are traveling on paths prearranged by the Creator. None of them have rocket engines to push them through space. Yet each moves steadily on, with some invisible force that scientists call momentum. Christians call it the power of God.

This cosmic show goes on over our heads each night in God's theater. Each production is flawless, with precision and detail that would put a planetarium projector to shame.

The director of all this is our God. He's the One that created us and sent a Son to redeem us when we lost our perfection. He's the One that keeps on loving us even though we're the part of His creation that walked out on Him.

What Are Friends for, Anyway?

One's friends are that part of the human race with which one can be human.
— *George Santayana*

It wasn't because of his appearance. Frank was far from being unattractive. He was always clean and never had a hair out of place.

It wasn't because he was hard to get along with or had a temper. Frank never argued. He always did what he was told.

It wasn't that he was mentally slow. In fact, he could whip through math problems faster than anyone else in the class.

And it wasn't a matter of Frank being unwilling to help someone in need. Frank always did what he could to solve people's problems. It seemed like he was helping them with their schoolwork all day long.

But the fact remained: Frank just didn't have any real friends. Oh, he was popular enough. He had people around him all day long in school. But no one really treated Frank as just one of the guys. They all had their own group of friends, people with whom they could share a joke, or a lunch, or a disappointment. Frank was never part of any of the groups. They respected Frank. They marveled at his ability, but they just didn't treat him like everyone else.

Maybe it was because of the way Frank treated them. He never shared how he felt. He never told anyone about his own joys and frustrations. He never asked for any kind of help. He didn't understand that friends do more than just react to the superficial parts of life.

Friendship goes deeper. It means a commitment to help and to be helped, to share both the joys and the sorrows. A person needs a friend, not just to get help from, but also to have someone to help. When a person chooses a friend, it's not just because he wants someone to aid him or amuse him. He chooses friends that he, in turn, can aid and amuse. He needs to feel that he is enriching the life of someone else. Perhaps many of us are too concerned about whether or not we're impressing those that we want to be our friends. As a result, we don't realize that they need to feel as though they are contributing to our lives also.

A life of only receiving is a very hollow life. So is a life of only giving. Friendship is a two-way street.

Maybe Frank can be forgiven for the way he acted with others around him. He simply was never programmed to ask for help. Few computers are.

God's Eyes Never Blink

I see the better way and approve it; I follow the worse.

— Ovid

God looked across the sea of people on His earth to a particular spot in a small town. It was late in the evening. He watched as a boy named Larry used red spray paint to disfigure Mr. Franklin's gas pumps. God's eyes focused on the boy's wide grin as he left the scene. He knew Larry's thoughts. The boy had done it to get even for being chased away earlier in the day.

In the eyes of the police, the incident is a case between Larry and Mr. Franklin. But in the eyes of God, the incident is between Larry and God Himself. He has created Larry and given him the talents and opportunities to be His helper on earth. Larry has chosen to do otherwise.

A person's actions fall into two categories—selfish and selfless. Selfishness puts one's self first. It disregards the best interest of other people and of God's wishes. It's like taking God's gift of pure water and mixing it with ink.

Selflessness puts God, and therefore others, ahead of self. It's called love. It's God's intent for people. It's like taking God's gift of pure water and sharing it with someone who thirsts.

People have a way of passing off their decisions to sin with the excuse, "I'm only human." That's true. Try as we might we still sin. Humans don't achieve perfection on earth. But to merely pass off sin in such a manner puts the blame on the Creator rather than the sinner.

Doing this is like the mother who walked into a storekeeper's shop to complain. "I sent my little boy over to buy two pounds of fresh cookies," she said. "He paid for two pounds but only came back home with one pound. Something must be wrong with your scale."

"My scale is accurate," replied the storekeeper. "Have you weighed your little boy?"

The woman tried to place the blame on the scale. People try to place it on God's creative hand. In both cases, the blame is misplaced.

The decision to sin is ours. We choose to do what we want regardless of the impact it may have upon God's creation. We disappoint God with our words and actions.

Our sin separates us from God. But because of Christ's death we are brought back to God. "You are to think of yourselves as dead, so far as sin is concerned, but *living in fellowship* with God through Christ Jesus" (Romans 6:11; italics added).

Our sins still offend God. They are a direct attack upon His authority. But because of Christ they no longer separate us from God. He still loves us. He still cares for us.

In view of this union with God through Christ, we are enabled to live a life of thanks to Him. We show our thanks by doing what we can to spread that love of God to the people we meet. We'll continue to sin and to disappoint God. But we start out fresh again through faith, with new opportunities to show the love of God in Christ.

Easy Streets and Difficult Paths

We have to learn that personal suffering is a more effective key, a more rewarding principle for exploring the world in thought and action than personal fortune.

— Dietrich Bonhoeffer

With each passing year new luxury items designed to lighten our work load are invented. Within a few years many of these inventions are no longer considered luxuries. They're necessities, something we "just have to have."

It's been estimated that an average American today has the equivalent of at least 400 servants working for him. While that estimate seems illogically high, consider what the average American has at his or her command. Think of how many servants would be needed to try to get us from place to place like an automobile does. Add to that the number of servants it would take to keep fires going during cold weather in order to keep us warm like a modern boiler or furnace does. The artificial lighting in our homes and schools couldn't be equaled by the use of torches or lamps. But it would take dozens of people to try to arrange suitable nonelectric lighting for each place we would require it during the day. The fast food restaurants illustrate the number of people that are needed in the production of the food we eat. Dozens of other modern-day inventions replace the hundreds of people needed to try to duplicate them.

Most people living in technologically developed countries have more luxuries than the richest of the ancient kings. Television, cars, and electric lights were unheard of by even the wealthiest rulers of not too long ago.

While such luxuries make life easier, they don't necessarily make it better. When life is soft it may become difficult for us to see God. We may get swept along by the fast-moving current of technology. But when things become a little rougher and filled with some pain, our eyes more readily look to Him. We become more keenly aware of how essential His guiding hand is.

For example, sickness or a misunderstanding with a cherished friend may lead us to rethink some things we had taken for granted.

In so doing, we are led to more clearly understand the blessing we have been given.

When God sends us disappointments in whatever form they take, He is doing so to instruct us. He doesn't want us to mindlessly accept our good fortune. He wants us to accept His blessings with gratitude so that our attitude can be one of sharing. Setbacks need to be seen as God working in our life's situations to mold us. Through them, we become more fit to be of service in His kingdom.

Problems, Perplexities, and Parents

Before I got married I had six theories about bringing up children; now I have six children and no theories.
— John Wilmot

"Are you trying to drive me crazy?" "Is that all? I thought your problem was something important." "When I was your age, we didn't do that." "How could you do this to me?" "Oh, don't worry about it."

These are some common responses by parents to their teenagers. Words such as these block meaningful discussion. They hurt.

When a young person looks for a solution to a problem, an obvious place to begin is with a parent. Being older and having had some experience, a parent is a logical choice. One of the big differences between a parent and a teen is experience. Parents have lived through many of the situations that teens are facing for the first time. Parents can see from a broader perspective. They have learned things about life that are worth sharing. Their advice should be sought and respected. Parents are usually very helpful.

But sometimes they aren't. Usually this isn't because of a lack of concern. Many times parents simply don't know what to say or how to react. Many parents try their best to help their children with good advice through tough times, but sometimes they just don't know what should be said or done.

As a result, their responses are sometimes inappropriate. Their desire to help makes them prey to certain traps. Often these pitfalls reflect the way their parents reacted to them when they had problems. They might resort to a long lecture, thinking that the more words they speak, the more helpful they are. They might give advice that is so general that it has no specific application to the problem. They might try to minimize the importance of the problem. In each instance, their advice isn't very helpful. But it's not because the parent isn't trying.

For example, if a girl tells her mother that she has just broken up with her boyfriend, the mother will be hard pressed to say anything of immediate comfort. The mother sees her daughter depressed and wants to help. But she isn't sure what to say. She will probably end up saying something like, "Oh, he wasn't good enough for you anyway," or, "Don't worry, there'll be plenty of other guys." Perhaps her response will be, "You've got your whole life ahead of you. Why be so depressed?"

In each case, the mother's words probably won't do much good. Maybe there was nothing she could have said that would have helped her daughter feel better right away. Some things just take time and trust. Perhaps the mother simply being there was helpful to the girl.

Parents have a difficult job in knowing what to do about their children's problems. Parents, of course, are people too. They make mistakes. They haven't been parents all their lives. They are learning too. Parents have the same feelings of inadequacy and awkwardness as their children.

Mothers and fathers have a lot to offer their children, but miracles aren't within their power. They need to be understood by their children when their advice or reaction isn't helpful. More is accomplished when teens are patient with their parents. Young people need to pray for their parents and with them. Both parents and teens can trust that with time, problems will be resolved. God will see to that.

This Old House

Ah, but a man's reach should exceed his grasp,
Or what's a heaven for?

— Robert Browning

There it was, the house in which he grew up. Up in the top corner was his bedroom. For years he had looked out of that window to see what the day, and the future, might bring. Now as a visitor

30 years later, he was looking up at the window to see what the past had brought. They had been good years. It was a good place to spend a childhood.

Down the road a mile was his former high school. His memories of it were fond, if maybe a little embarrassing. He remembered what a shy, skinny kid he had been. For some reason it flashed back through his mind how nervous he got whenever pretty Angie Fisher would talk to him in English class. But as time went on he got less shy. Why, he had even gotten up enough nerve once to ask one of Angie's friends out for a date. Those four years of high school raced by quickly.

After graduation he left home for college. After college he found a job in another town, and a few years later he married.

He recalled how tough it was to leave home back then. He really didn't want to abandon its security. But he knew that he had to go on with his life. He couldn't stay there forever. He had to venture out on his own at some point. Growing up meant making changes.

Changes are a necessary part of life. Some of them are easy to make. Many of them are not. At times we want to avoid the uncertainty they bring. We feel it's easier to retreat into the safety of doing things as we have in the past.

But if we're going to grow up, we need to take on challenges. We need to shrug off the fears we have about changes. For example, the thought of changing the school we attend may be worrisome. We may wish we didn't have to leave the security and familiarity of our previous school. Yet if we're going to further our formal education, at some point we have to start at a new school. Once we begin, we find out it's not nearly as scary as we had anticipated.

There's a joke about a football coach who wanted to see how much his third-string subs had learned from his coaching. He said to one, "Sam, pretend we've got the ball on the opponent's five-yard line. There's time for only one more play. What would you do?"

Sam thought for a moment and replied, "Well, coach, if the ball was on the five-yard line, I'd move to the end of the bench so I could see better."

Sam's answer indicates how he feels about himself. He seems to lack confidence. He's told himself that he won't be put into the game. In fact, he appears to be unwilling to get into it. He's afraid to make a change, afraid to try something more challenging.

Christians don't need to feel this way about opportunities that present themselves. With God's promise of help, we can confront the challenges that life brings. We can "get into the game," knowing that God will help us accomplish what is best for us. Changes no longer need to be avoided.

The Road Not Taken

Don't keep forever on the public road, going only where others have gone. Leave the beaten path occasionally and drive into the woods.
— Alexander Graham Bell

The ball spiraled toward the receiver's waiting hands. Mark, the cornerback, wouldn't have enough time to knock down the pass. But he would be in perfect position to give the receiver a bone-jarring jolt as soon as he caught it. After all, this is a tough sport, thought Mark. Guys shouldn't play football if they can't take it. Besides, the opponent waiting for the ball was the same one that had caught a touchdown pass earlier. But now he was standing next to the sideline waiting for the ball, vulnerable. Mark's momentum was taking him straight for the motionless target. All Mark had to do was lower his helmet and drive straight into his opponent. The guy might catch the ball, but he'd have to pay the price.

The moment of vengeance had arrived. The ball was caught, and Mark approached. But he didn't cause a collision. He didn't try to blast the receiver off the face of the earth. All he did was push him out of bounds. It was that simple. No one got hurt and no one got revenge. The play simply ended after a gain of a few yards.

Beth was pleased when she opened the note and read that she was invited to Carol's party on Saturday night. A lot of the popular kids would be there. Getting the invitation was a kind of status symbol in itself. Beth felt good to be included. But those parties usually weren't much fun. Oh, there'd be plenty of laughter and talking and put downs of one another, but not really all that much fun. It seemed to Beth that the kids were putting on acts. They all appeared to be pretending to have a good time, trying to act mature, trying to be cool. She wasn't sure how many of the kids really enjoyed themselves, but she didn't think there were all that many. Most of them went to these parties, she suspected, just because it was the thing to do.

As Saturday night drew nearer, Beth's friends assured her that she should go. Why, she just *had* to go. Anyway, what else was there to do?

Saturday night came and went. Beth stayed home. She did some homework, watched some television, and played a game with her parents and younger brother. She enjoyed herself.

Neither Mark nor Beth fits the mold. Neither of them did what they had a chance to do. Neither of them did the expected.

There are others like them. A prominent lawyer gives up his well-paying practice to give low-cost legal aid to poor families. A businessman takes time out from an already busy schedule to help an elderly neighbor paint his house. A high school senior baby-sits for her own little brother for free rather than baby-sit somewhere else for pay.

People such as these seem to have a vision. They are able to see past the obstacles of revenge, peer pressure, laziness, and greed. They see better than most what God has in mind for them. They're willing to travel the road that isn't so often traveled. It's a road seldom used but one that is very rewarding.

This Time Forever

On the earth the broken arcs; in the heaven, a perfect round.
— Robert Browning

A city boy on his first visit to a farm was taken to see the lambs. After some initial fear, he finally got up the courage to pet one of them. Greatly surprised at how it felt, he exclaimed, "Wow, they make those things out of blankets."

It's normal for people to explain what is unknown to them in terms of what they know and have experienced. For instance, earlier in our country's history some American Indians who had never seen a gun called it a firestick. They used the known to explain the unknown.

We do that same sort of thing when we picture heaven. We think about heaven in terms of fleecy clouds, golden buildings, and beautiful music. We use the known to give us a picture of the unknown. We are so settled into the words, sights, and experiences of this world that it becomes difficult to break away. But heaven must be drastically superior to our present experiences — or it wouldn't be heaven.

Certain segments of our life are filled with joy. We are thrilled by a good movie. We are ecstatic about an award. We are warmed by the companionship of a cute puppy. But each of these experiences is only a short rest from the labors of this world. They come to an end. And since we know they will come to an end, our joy is limited even at the moment of enjoyment.

But heaven carries with it the absence of time limits. All our lives we labor within the restraints imposed by our sinful nature. But one day those limits will be removed. Our trust in the work of Christ to overcome our sinfulness will be validated. The unreachable will become reachable. The temporary rest will become permanent.

Presently we worry about fitting in with certain groups. We hope we are good enough to make the team. We hope we can gain the acceptance of our friends. We hope our teachers consider us worthy of a good grade. But in heaven those worries about belonging cease. We will begin to realize that we have been personally accepted by God because of the actions of Christ for us. We'll be in heaven by invitation. We'll be permanent members of His select group.

As long as we're on this earth, we'll continue to think of heaven by using our earthly images. That's all we can do on this side of the grave. But some day our eyes will open. The inconceivable will then become conceivable.

In Closing

Life is not a problem to be solved but a reality to be experienced.
—Søren Kierkegaard

One summer day a first-grade teacher met a boy from her previous class in a store. "I'm glad you're going on to the second grade, Dale, and I'm sure you are smart enough to be there."

Dale looked down at his feet and replied, "I'm glad too, Ma'am, but I'm awfully sorry you couldn't make it."

Life moves on at an alarmingly quick rate. Circumstances change daily. Some people move out of our life and others move in. Each year brings new mountains to climb, to slip on and slide down, and to try again and again, eventually to conquer. The problems that seemed so insurmountable to us as small children now rekindle fond memories of past achievements. And the problems we face now will someday be recalled in a similar way.

Life is a new challenge each day. There are always old problems to solve and new discoveries to be made. Each passing day is another confirmation of God working in us.

The preceding pages have been an attempt to illustrate how God works in us and how we can therefore work among His people. The emphasis has been on a God that loves us in Christ despite our frailties and failures. The result of this love for us is a life that is exciting, challenging, and rewarding. It's a life worth living to its fullest.